The Mirror Principle

KJB

First published in 2018 by Publish Wiz

Copyright © 2018 KJB

All rights reserved. This book or any portion thereof may not be reproduced or used in any manner whatsoever without the express written permission of the publisher except for the use of brief quotations in a book review.

ISBN: 978-1-7179-7006-0

www.themirrorprinciple.org

Publish Wiz

P.O. Box CT2226

Cantonments Accra, Ghana

Email: info@publishwiz.com

www.publishwiz.com

To Dad and Mum, who gave me strong values, the support to stand on my feet, and sacrificed part of their lives to make mine prosperous.

To Elena, my complete bundle of inspiration, love, laughter, and creativity. Also, thank you for being the perfect mirror for our daughter.

Contents

Acknowledgements i

Preface ii

1 The Mirror 1

2 The Seed 29

3 The Mind 56

4 Mirror Principle: The Seed, The Mirror and The Mind 101

5 The Mirror Principle In Action 147

6 Mirror Cleaners and Mirror Blurrers 177

7 The Mirror Principle And An Organization 236

8 The Mirror Principle And A Nation 267

9 The Mirror Principle and Children 310

10 The Conclusion Of The Matter 340

Acknowledgements

Thanks to Ian McMonagle, Alina Budina, Ryan Mulligan, St. Albans New Cadets, Myles Munroe, Sarita Patel, Uche Iloka, Kamba Abudu, and of course Idris, Teslim, Sheffy and Zainab. May all your candles continue to burn bright.

KJB

Preface

On These Pages ….

This is a simple book. Just as the best things in life are free, so are the most powerful truths always simple. My father had a number of wise quotes that he shared with us from time to time. One of them is the phrase "there is nothing new under the sun"; how true. Pause and recall every event, word of wisdom or invention that you have ever known. If you give it some thought you will find an undeniable connection to a concept that has already existed. The amazing computer once surfaced in the primeval form of the Babylonian abacus; today's video games are a classy adaptation of the shadow puppet creations of ancient Chinese masters; money existed as property before the concept of paper currency; today's wonder medications were once conjured and administered by Egyptian herbalists several centuries ago.

It is true that we discover new things, but the truth is they have always existed. Discovery is never ending; but truth is constant. Humans are blessed with the uncanny ability to view a single concept in a million different ways. The end results are widely different, but the concept is one and the same. This book delivers a simple truth into your hands. It is a modern depiction of a timeless concept about the human journey. It could present to you a different perspective to life, but at the core of its message is the same truth that has been passed down from generation to generation; revealed at different dispensations of human history; taught by the sages of each era. Truth will not be truth if it changes with time. Truth has many expressions but only one face. This book is one of those expressions for this modern era.

Whether you are an artist aspiring to greater heights, a new parent experiencing the thrills of raising a newborn, a homeless man abandoned on the cold streets of depravity, a captain of a soaring industry, an elderly woman now in your latter years or a teenager with no clue what you want to become, this book brings a valuable view into your life. It delivers a fresh insight on the essence of living and opens your heart to endless possibilities. It takes some of the most common things we use in our everyday lives and relates these things to the paths of fulfilment that we all seek. On these pages we are suddenly faced with everyday objects, which we previously ignored but whose values come alive in a most sublime way. We are introduced to Mirrors, Seeds and Thoughts. Soon we see how a timeless principle uses these three instruments to affect our lives in significant ways.

The Mirror Principle begins with an object that was never invented by man; The Mirror. An object whose uses exceed the vain functions it is often associated with today. The mirror is a unique item that first surfaced as pools of still water bearing our reflections. Encircled in mystic and history, the mirror and its true strength are unveiled in the first chapter. On the next two chapters you find two common phenomena portrayed in a light perhaps unknown to you. The first is the seed, portrayed as a powerful allegory to the human purpose. The next, on the third chapter, is the human mind exposed in all its beauty.

It is only in the fourth chapter you begin to piece together the remarkable connection between these three things. In this chapter you discover how these three things form the very foundation upon which your life is founded. We come face to face with The Mirror Principle.

In chapter five, we observe this principle in the lives of people around the world; rich or poor; successful or unaccomplished; famous or uncelebrated. We realize the subtle differences in our lives, each one centred on The Mirror

Principle. We discover how the outcomes of our lives, varied as they may be, are all ordered by this unchanging concept. We learn more about the principle and in so doing we become masters of the principle. We soon discover that masters of the principle belong to a privileged group of human beings who have unearthed the way to live life to its fullest. On these pages, we come to understand the difference between accomplishment and fulfilment. We find that not all success is desired. We discover the kind of success we desire.

The sixth chapter follows closely from the real-life examples in the preceding chapters. It speaks about tools and practices that either open or shut the doors to the fulfilment we all seek.

The chapters that follow are dedicated to the principle, and how it is applied in different contexts. It touches on some vital aspects of our lives, and how the mastering of The Mirror Principle could help in getting us to the pinnacle of success.

In a sense this book shows that The Mirror Principle is a law that we are bound by; a race that we must run but a race that we can win. This law, The Mirror Principle, gives us the hope that we surely need; exposes in simple terms the truth that sets us free. I hope you find this worthwhile.

1 The Mirror

The Mirror: From An Ancient Mystery To A Modern Necessity.

We begin in 2060 BC. Jia Xian wiped the sweat off his brows. Drops of perspiration were slowly rolling down his cheeks. He cared less. He knew that the anguish of the moment could not compare with the joy of his approaching conquest. The sun was high up in the sky now and so were the expectations of his Emperor. For thirteen days Jia had lived on rations of millet and rice wine. He yearned for fresh water but around these enclosed hills of Aihua where he had laid ambush, clean water was as rare as hen's teeth.

He contemplated sitting upright to pacify his blood-starved veins. For hours he had lain flat on his belly with his neck lurched to get a view of his oncoming prey. "Stay still Jia!" he cautioned himself. It was too risky to indulge now. He could hear his target a few steps away on the valley below. From the sounds of the horses' hooves he could tell that there were two of them. One of them was whistling loudly; a trait Jia instantly recognised as becoming of a wise old man. He figured the second rider was merely a protégé. He would have to face two men, but Jia knew he had a weapon which counted for as much as a dozen men; the element of surprise. He clutched on to the bronze dagger tied to his hips. It was time.

Swiftly, he emerged from the boulders. He jumped on the horse of the second horseman. Amidst the whining of the horse, Jia grabbed the horse rider by the neck and slit his throat leaving him to crash to the sands. As he had anticipated, the leading horseman turned around. As cleanly as he had taken the life of the second horseman he spun his dagger with deadly force aiming at his target's chest. The leading horseman yelled loudly and fell to the ground. As though believing his shot could never miss, Jia jumped down from the horse and headed straight for the leading horseman's handbag. He looked in it and saw his prize. Then he whistled for his horse. As the loyal creature came trotting from the caves, Jia looked over at the two lifeless bodies adorning the sands. He marvelled at the precision of his own aim. The conquest was easier than he had imagined.

Back at the awe-inspiring palace of Emperor Yu, the wise council of the Xia dynasty gathered to discuss with the great Emperor. Jia, the Emperor's most trusted warrior stood by the king. He savoured the moment. As Emperor Yu chronicled the stories of his triumphs along the Yellow River, Jia's mind flashed back to the object he had delivered to the Emperor moments ago. The prize was a strange one. Not that Jia had ever seen anything like it before, but it looked too simple to warrant sleepless nights for the great Emperor. But he knew better than to berate the Emperor's judgements. His years of working with the Emperor had taught him that in the end the Emperor was always right.

At first sight it was a fine piece of obsidian glass just about the size of Jia's head. The rear of the glass was polished with some kind of fine substance. Underneath the glass, a text written in a strange language was engraved. In this glass, Jia could see the reflection of himself. It reminded him of how as a child, he would stare endlessly at his reflection in a pool of still water. This piece of glass seemed like all the reflections of the river locked in one small box. It looked like a vain object of beauty. If he did not know the Emperor well enough he would have presumed the glass was a gift for one of his wives. But there was something more to this glass that caught the reverence of the Emperor. Whatever it was, Jia knew he had performed his own task. His calling was to deliver the object of Emperor Yu's desires into the Emperor's hands. The use of such objects or their hidden powers was entirely the preserve of the Emperor and his wise council.

KJB

***

Now the year is 1000 BC. We are in the nation of Tibet.

A swift breeze from the Changye River blows across the Yarhung valley in Guge, western Tibet. Sonam Drup had always looked forward to this day with unease and contemplation. His life and indeed the destiny of the Guge people rested on the outcome of the ritual he was about to undertake. Sonam was only 16 years old. Yet the sudden demise of his father, Choden Drup, the ordained Master of the Nechung Temple meant that his gifts had to be tested. Like many before him, his ascension to the throne of Master had to be proven under the watchful eyes of the king.

As his servants tidied up his praying room, Sonam's mind flashed back to all the lessons his great father had taught him. "The gift is useless until the bearer understands its meaning", his father would say. Sonam was born with special eyes, which he inherited from his father's. These special eyes could read the sayings of the thugs-kyi melong; stainless mirrors of great significance to the people of Guge. Through the thugs-kyi melong, the ordained Master invokes the spirit of Dorje Yudronma, the feared but compassionate protector of Guge.

Sonam could read colours and forms from the mirrors. On a few occasions, he had interpreted the letters inscribed on the mirrors; answers to deep questions that bothered the minds of his people. Now he had been called upon to perform a healing ritual. The king's only son had been bitten by a wild dog and was stricken with rabies. If Sonam's rituals cure the illness, then no other stage would be needed to prove that the mantle of the ordained Master had passed on from father to son.

Two of the king's servants stretchered the sick boy into Sonam's chambers. They reverently laid him on the floor and Sonam set to his task. He lifted up one of the thugs-kyi melong, a small mirror, and passed it over the boy's body. He watched the colour changes on the mirror for several minutes. He stopped at a spot just above the boy's knee. "The seat of the illness", he thought to himself. Next he poured some water over a large mirror, which seemed to reflect a sacred image. He sprinkled some red sindhura powder on the mirror and made a light mixture with his fingers. "Sacred water", he said to himself, recalling the words of his father. He laid the large mirror back down. He grabbed dadar; an arrow topped with a mirror and yellow, red and white ribbons. Swiftly, he struck the tip of the arrow into the boy's inner thigh. For the first time, the boy cried out in agony as blood and puss spurted out of his thigh. As though oblivious to the agony of his patient, Sonam scooped out some of the mixture he had prepared. He massaged the mixture into the open wound and washed off his hands in a bowl of water.

As though acting out a well-rehearsed script, two of Sonam's servants came to his side and started to tidy up. To them the washing of the hands signified the end of the ritual. Sonam stood up, dried his hands on his skirt and left the room. A calming feeling swept through him. Surely, the healing powers of the mirror had come good again. He knew he had just saved the life of the heir to the throne of Guge.

***

The year is now 56 AD. Location is Ephesus, now in modern day Turkey.

Paul of Tarsus sat at his desk pondering over his next words. Over the last seven years his teachings and letters were almost as valuable to his followers as the air they breathe. Ardent disciples of Paul believed in the divinity of every word he spoke. Whether they lived in Rome, Jerusalem, Greece or Mesopotamia, Paul of Tarsus was regarded by thousands as the hand of God on earth; the torchbearer of the Christian faith.

In Paul's mind, he was nothing but a mere disciple; an ordinary tentmaker who made ends meet by offering his tent making skills to as many as would pay for it while he travelled several hundreds of miles on foot and by sea. Wearied from his many sojourns, persecution by the authorities and painful ordeals in the hands of Roman soldiers, Paul had endured unspeakable hardships. And there was an even worse pain he bore; the mental torture.

Every day, he woke up with a constant reminder of the life he had sacrificed to fulfil his calling. Born to parents who were honorary citizens of Rome, he was the sole heir to a thriving tent making franchise. Paul was supposed to be a man of affluence and power. Now in his fifties, a man of wealth and power he was; not in the worldly sense of merchandise and palaces but in the higher realms of the spiritual world. In Christendom, Paul was a stalwart. He was gifted with the rare ability to discern spiritual truths. He understood the undercurrents of the spiritual world. Since becoming a devout follower, he had risen through the ranks of teachers with his uncanny ability to unveil truths that brought comfort and strength to the body of Christ. He was referred to in some quarters as the Pen of the Divine Hand.

Two young men were sleeping on the bed two feet away from Paul's desk that night. One of the young men stirred noisily, appeared to be half awake for a moment and then fell back into sleep. Paul could see him clearly from across his desk even though the room was only dimly lit by Paul's reading lamp. He stared at both men for a minute. The two men were Titus and Timothy, sworn followers of Paul. They had both toiled with Paul on many of his journeys; his trusted compadres. "The future of Christianity", Paul whispered under his breath, "the true vessels of honour", he thought. Tomorrow, Titus would set sail to Corinth with an epistle from Paul. Paul knew the church at Corinth was at the brink of annihilation. The authorities were hunting down believers of the outlawed Christian faith. Even Paul would admit that fierce persecution could coerce the most devout of disciples to deny the things they believed to be true. It was Paul's calling to bring them hope and guidance.

Paul's mind switched back to the epistle that was now forming on his desk. The letter to the church at Corinth was almost ready. Paul was convinced that his writings carried an inspired message; a message that could set the faithful at Corinth on the right path for years to come. In the epistle, he had rendered his most potent words yet on the subject of love. "And though I have all faith, so that I could remove mountains but have not love, I am nothing", he had written. He sensed that the night was now far spent. He resisted the temptation to put out the light. From years of experience, he knew that a ray of revelation was on its way. The divine hand was at work; he could feel it.

He dropped his pen and gazed into the object that hung on the wall in front of him. It was a wooden framed mirror Paul had received from an old friend Ananais. He indulged in an old habit of running his fingers through his thick beards as he stared at his own tired reflection in the mirror. It reminded him again of how far he had come. From living an ordinary life of survival to living a life that carried a higher meaning; a life where he could sit above human struggles; a life where the world made more sense. Suddenly it dawned on him. The words struck him as though the Divine Hand itself wrote them. Blepomen gar arti di esoptrou en ainigmati. In English, "For now we look through a glass, darkly".

"This is it", Paul thought. In the dim light, as we look in the mirror, we see imperfection. What we need is more light. When there is more enlightenment, then we can see the vision more clearly; a perfect reflection. Paul stayed up for a few more hours as he pondered on the depth of these words. "A potent revelation which has the power to change the world as we know it", the great teacher thought to himself.

***

Now, it is late spring in the year 2005. The scene is a middle class apartment block, Blackheath, South London, United Kingdom. Joanna rolled out of bed. There had not been many times she had got out of bed fully awake. Usually she would scramble out of bed like a one-eyed monster under the influence of some kind of overdose. Then she would make the awkward fidgety walk to the bathroom. Not this time though. 6.15 a.m. One of the rare times she had beaten the alarm clock to it. "It has to be the anxiety", she reasoned. She ran her hands through her hair as she let out a huge yawn. "Got an extra thirty minutes to prepare", she thought to herself.

Joanna was interviewing for a job that previously existed only in her dreams. As she made for the bathroom, the thought of it made her shudder. It was certainly one of those fright-filled mornings. Was she good enough? Did she have the skills the recruiters wanted? What was it about her phone interview that they liked enough to shortlist her? All these questions raced through Joanna's mind. Not even the warm shower, her ever-reliable stress reliever, could stop the doubts from creeping in. But unlike the last interview, she was certainly more composed this time. "Nerves are normal on days like this", she reminded herself.

The bright rays of sunlight flooded the room. Joanna stood in front of the bedroom mirror as she dressed up. She commended herself for picking the outfit that she had on. She thought she looked very smart; dressed for the part. Her well-fitting charcoal suit subtly accentuated her slight curves. She cut the figure of a powerful woman. Her simple pearl necklace, the three-inch high suede shoes and leather handbag complemented her smart look. The anxiety she woke up with

The Mirror Principle

was still there but now it felt somewhat different. The self-doubts had vanished. She was feeling a burst of positive energy; feeling like she was ready to take on the whole world. Now she was exuding confidence.

For a moment, her mind drifted back to the last interview she had. "What a stark contrast", she thought. The night before that interview, she had yielded to the prodding of her friends. They wanted her to join them for the U2 concert. "It will be a quiet one and you should be relaxing in bed before midnight", the girls had assured. Joanna pretended to believe that; looking forward to a quiet night with the girls was like expecting a game of boxing without punches. At midnight, Joanna and her girls were still caught up in the U2 hysteria. The shots of vodka and flaming Lamborghini cocktails lasted well into the early hours of the morning.

Later that morning, Joanna had woken up 45 minutes before her interview appointment. She got out of bed with a banging head, and no clue what to wear and no time to shower. A glance at the mirror before she dashed out of her flat did not help. In fact, she wished she had never looked in the mirror. She looked like a female heavyweight boxer who had just had a bad fight. The image tormented her all through the interview. She flunked the easiest of questions, and she could swear her interviewers could smell the whiff of alcohol sweeping through the room anytime she uttered a word. In the end as Joanna had expected, she got a swift response from the recruiter saying they didn't think she was right for the role.

Today was different. As she looked in that mirror, she saw a competent professional. Buoyed by her vast experience in the field she felt secure. She saw in herself an achiever; a prized asset to any company she worked for; a lady in control of things around her. She was in cruise control.

***

Now it is May 13th, 2011. Downtown Seattle, Washington, USA.

Sarah took another look at her watch. It was 7.50pm. She had 10 minutes left; the exact time it would take her to walk down from the train station to the hotel. She looked at the couple sitting opposite her. They were sweating profusely and seemed every bit as agitated as she was. "Maybe they have an important appointment to catch like me", she thought. If only she had listened to her gut feeling. She clearly had a premonition that there will be delays. "Public transportation is never 100 percent", she had warned herself two hours ago. That was before she decided to indulge in a chat with Mike her boss about some office work that could have waited until the next day. Mike had engaged her in one of his endless lectures about the future of life insurance. By the time he was done Sarah was at the mercy of the train services.

She had a big night ahead. This dinner was more than a romantic night out with Stuart her boyfriend. She was meeting with Stuart's mother and sister for the first time tonight. "Lateness is not an option. Neither is looking scruffy", she thought biting her lips; a sign of irritation. This was not how she had planned the night. The plan was to arrive downtown by 6pm, freshen up, and drive herself to the Edgewater Hotel. At the hotel, she would meet Stuart and they would both wait for his folks to join them at the dinner table by 8pm. The train had been stuck on the tracks for well over an hour. "No more going home", she thought, her teeth still biting firmly on her lips. "No more driving to the hotel". And even worse, there was not even a chance to freshen up.

She unzipped her bag and reached for her make up kit. "Aha, great", she cursed and sighed in one breath. It was one of those days she had forgotten her hand mirror. The night was not getting any better. She was not only going to be late, she was going to show up looking like death. Thick sweat was forming all over her face. She had never longed more for a restroom as she did now. Something was upsetting her nostrils. She was sneezing incessantly.

The train began to move slowly. The voice over the PA system, blurting out assurances that the delay was over, did nothing to change the mood of the disillusioned passengers. As the train hurtled to a halt at Seattle Westlake station, Sarah made her way to the door. She wriggled through an unfriendly crowd and lunged out. She headed for the adjoining street approaching the hotel. "Gosh! Where is a mirror when you need one", she thought as she walked past the hotel reception and towards the waterside area where Stuart and his folks would be waiting.

She was fifteen minutes late. Just as she contemplated making a dash for the restroom, there was Stuart with a broad smile, waving her to come on over. By his side were two stylishly dressed, smiling and confident looking women. Sarah tried to signal Stuart that she was not comfortable and needed to use the restroom but he did not notice. Stuart was a typical happy-go-lucky character. Knowing him, he would hardly be bothered if she appeared as mangy as a coal worker in Goonyella. To him, she was always beautiful. "But not to these two", she thought. "They are probably taking down notes".

She apologised for being late. She tried to help Stuart to break the ice but her unease was growing. "My hair must be all over the place", she thought "and what's that feeling in my nose? My makeup must be screwed up too. I must look horrible. I must end this misery".

"Sorry guys, I hate to be discourteous but excuse me. I need to use the ladies", she exclaimed, her voice hinting at her discomfort.

The thought of glancing at a mirror felt like a million dollars to her now. She realised how precious a mirror was in the life of a woman. As she escaped into the ladies, she moved swiftly for the mirror. She stared at herself. Sarah was startled by her own tidy reflection. She looked as though she had freshened up from home. And no, there was nothing in her nose. Her hair was intact. Her makeup was unscathed. She smiled. All of the ruffling on the train, sweaty walk and tortuous sneezing had left her thinking she looked like death. Her thoughts had played tricks on her. She bit her lips again, this time not in disgust but in jest of how she had thought the worst of herself. "Now bring on the night", she thought.

She got out her makeup kit and slicked up her looks. Sarah was now smiling in relief as her confidence returned. Now she was ready to chum around, drink and chat freely with Stuart's folks.

As she sat back at the table, she felt at ease. Sarah was now assured that she was not making a fool of herself. Not that

Stuart cared or noticed any changes, but to Sarah, the relief was priceless.

***

Finally we arrive to July 5th 2010. 8.35am, Parkview suite, The Ritz, Central Park, New York.

"Will you need anything else, sir?" The stewardess asked with a trained smile.

"No. That would be all for now", replied the polished, clean shaven man. He walked across the bedroom and reached for a tie. Then he made for the giant-sized mirror. As he had done deep into the previous night, he let the tunes from the iPod station sift through from the study. Coldplay's Fix You set a melancholic ambience around the Parkview suite. His calm mien almost betrayed the significance of the morning.

Robert Parsons, CEO of the multi-billion dollar Parsons Media Empire was a man on the verge of history. Eight years ago, he inherited a family business that spanned six generations. Parsons News Incorporated had always been a success story. America's number two media organisation had built its vast wealth on the strong credentials of solid ethics and social responsibility. Three years ago, tragedy struck. Facts emerged that some key members of the Parsons executive committee had uncovered and withheld evidence surrounding a high profile criminal case. Competitors and politicians alike fed on the scandal like hoggish vultures. Parsons Inc lost credibility. It relinquished its once enviable position as the nation's foremost media house. Market share was on a free fall. Share prices crashed even faster.

Robert and his team of dedicated advisers did not balk under the intense pressure. Showing true leadership qualities, he fished out the bad eggs and restructured the company. In the last three years he had restored Parsons Inc to some level of decency. Now, just when things were turning on its head Robert had something new to worry about. Another media giant was scheming a hostile takeover. The bid had gained so much momentum that the company was divided. To some, Parsons Inc needed to merge for survival. To others, the unique vision of Parsons Inc was at stake. The big decision lay on the table of one person alone; Robert Parsons. In a few hours, he would submit his decision on the matter. He had barely slept. His decision could potentially affect tens of thousands of families. Now he wished his father was there with him to give him some words of advice.

Robert adjusted his tie and slipped into his jacket. He inspected his hair and took one last glance at himself. His eyes caught the gold brooch that was pinned to the lapel of his suit. For the next five minutes, Robert's mind shuttled between the glittering brooch and thoughts of the deep meanings that the ornament connoted. The brooch was more than a mere piece of jewellery. It bore the logo of Parsons Inc; a symbol of all that Parsons Inc stood for. This symbol had passed through six generations; a message forged through time. Inscribed on the brooch was the image of a lion wielding a torch. The lion portrayed nobility, courage and power. The torch symbolized enlightenment.

Robert reminisced on when he was 16, and his father had explained the meaning of the company's logo. "It carries the essence of who we are", his father had said beaming with pride as he held up this same brooch. "The torch sheds light on society. It exposes the negatives and celebrates the positives. The lion exudes our strength; the resolve to brave the odds through good and bad times. The lion never backs down from a challenge".

"Yes, that was it".

Right in front of Robert was the reflection of what the company stood for. This was only a challenge. It was not in the character of Parsons Inc to fall apart under pressure. He knew at once what his decision was. Parsons Inc will not be sold. Nobody was getting sacked or getting their heads down. They had faced hurdles in the past, and they came through bigger and better. This was yet another battle and in true Parsons' fashion, they will triumph.

The Mirror: From An Ancient Mystery To A Modern Necessity

The mirror is perhaps the most undervalued invention of man's modern era. There is hardly any home without a mirror; hardly any human being that has not used one.

All throughout the existence of mankind, there has been an undeniable need for the mirror. Whether it was a mirror made out of obsidian glass in 6000 BC, or polished copper in ancient Egypt in 3000 BC, or silvered glass in Germany in the 1800s, the use of the mirror in our daily lives is astounding.

1. There are over a billion mirrors existing in today's world. Almost three quarters of these mirrors go unnoticed.
2. Mirrors form an essential part of vital devices like security systems, solar power generators, car rear and side view

mirrors, dental mirrors, cameras, televisions, telescopes, periscopes and video projectors.
3. The oldest mirrors are likely pools of dark stable water or water held in a vessel.
4. Most of the greatest artists have used mirrors in creating the most celebrated portraits in art history.
5. While designing the much-heralded Hand with the Reflecting Sphere, M. C. Escher used a mirror to view his surroundings including the view of places that his natural eyes could not see.
6. Mirrors, notably in the ancient times commanded great superstitious meanings. Mirrors were regarded amongst many wise councillors as the reflection of the soul. Mirrors were used as the ultimate tool in traditional witchcraft. It was said that when you break a mirror, you break a soul.
7. Many Buddhists believe that hanging a small circular mirror outside of the front door repels bad spirits.
8. Many Mayans, Aztecs, Egyptians, Indians and even modern-day Romanians use mirrors to ward off or trap the souls of evil spirits.
9. Scryers the feared diviners, use mirrors to peer into the mystic future. Many diviners still summon a person's soul by looking in a mirror in a dark room.

The Mirror Principle

Today, the use of the mirror is a mere ritual. Every day we use mirrors, and most times their usefulness goes unnoticed. Surprisingly amongst animals, only humans, elephants and dolphins are intelligent enough to recognise the image on the mirror as a reflection of themselves. To other animals, the mirror reflection is someone else. They see a rival, or in some cases a friend.

How often we tend to take the common things for granted. We sometimes undermine the basic necessities that exist in abundance whether it is the air we breathe, the water we consume or reflective surfaces. Let us pause for a moment and ponder. Imagine a world without mirrors. Think of what the world would look like without reflections or pictures. Transportation as we know it would not exist. The diagnosis of illness in vital parts of our bodies would be impossible. Space research would move at a tiny fraction of its present pace. Perhaps the most important bit of all is that we would barely have an assurance of how we look. Self-image is at the core of any human endeavour. Mirrors play a big part in this personal discovery. Every person acts according to the dictates of their self-image; every human dances to the drumbeats of what he or she thinks of himself. It is only after self-image is sorted, do we then focus our brains towards more productive ventures. To a very large extent, our self-image is hinged on the mental perception we have gained from mirrors. If mirrors did not exist we would have to depend on people's perception of us to create our self-image; the very substance of our being.

Sages Elixir

"In my life I have known many great painters. The Master of Painters is the Mirror".

Leonardo Da Vinci

In the fourteenth century and prior, when mirrors were made out of metal and stones, they were revered as mythical objects. They were sacred and divine. In today's world, mirrors have somewhat been reduced to objects of physical vanity. A clear illustration of this trend could be seen in the six tales told earlier. From Jia Xian in 2060 AD to Sonam Drup to Paul of Tarsus, Joanna, Sarah and Robert Parsons in 2010 AD, the mirror has carried invaluable significance. Through these years the mirror has conveyed many meanings. Although it has symbolized different things to the scientists and superstitious alike, we all agree on one thing: Mirrors never lie. They are yet the most sublime painters of physical reality.

Sages Elixir

"Beauty is truth's smile when she beholds her own face in a perfect Mirror".

Radindranath Tagore

One remarkable value of the mirror is its inherent ability to provide vision beyond the reach of our physical eyes. A clear example of this phenomenon in our everyday lives is demonstrated when we walk into a hair salon to be treated to a hairdo. With the use of mirrors, the hair stylist is able to provide us with visuals of our head. We even get to see behind our heads, which would ordinarily have been impossible to view. It is almost like turning your neck 360 degrees, and yet being able to see the back of your head.

Mirrors have the ability to increase the scope of our vision. Scientists and astronomers are able to see well into distant space with the aid of mirrors. When mirrors are intelligently assembled, there is a tremendous view that we can get of places that might be millions of miles away.

Then there are our car rides. On the road, we are faced with a lack of awareness for what is happening around the vehicle. Our vision only covers about a semi-circle radius at best. Automobile experts refer to this as the blind spot. There are many blind spots we face when driving, but mirrors help us cover many of these blind areas. The mirror gives us vision that we so desperately desire. With the aid of mirrors, we suddenly have a rear and side view, which makes us more aware of the things our physical eyes would not see. Then we are able to drive safer and avoid disastrous accidents. Could you imagine cars without mirrors? The horrific scenes we would be greeted with as road users crash into each other? Let us not even talk about the massive horn blaring cacophony that this would create. What this shows to us is the fact that a mirror is an integral part of human existence. Mirrors enhance the vision of the human eyes. A mirror assists us to see beyond; it is a third eye of some sort.

With the mirror, our vision is enlarged. Moreover, the mirror provides clarity to the little details within our vision. How often do we wake up running our fingers all over our eyes? To some of us, this has become a reflex action. We do this in a bid to clear our eyes of crusts that formed around our eyes when we slept. As though this were not enough, we almost habitually head for the bathroom mirror. Why do we do this? We are merely inspecting the eyes to ensure that all the crusts are gone. More often than not, you may find yourself picking at the eyes again as the mirror shows you that some stubborn crusts are still hidden in the corners of your eyes. This is a classic example of the detail that the mirror provides.

The Mirror Principle

While speaking of our eyes and its romance with the mirror, one quickly recalls the uneasy moments when some unwelcome particle finds its way into our eyes. This incident could last a tortuous few minutes. Specks of dust can be removed from other parts of our body with relative ease. You can search for the imposters with your eyes, spot them and flick them off your body. It is not so easy when the speck beats the eye's defence mechanism, and gets into your eyes. What do we do? Sometimes we reach for the mirror. Barely able to open our eyes for long periods of time, the mirror reveals the speck through our blinkered vision, and we get rid of the speck.

Through this simple action, another value of the mirror is unveiled. This value is the ability to help us identify where the issues lie. By using the reflective nature of the mirror, we have on numerous occasions identified the pain points, and gotten rid of the hitches. This also alludes to the story earlier told of Robert Parsons. He faced a dilemma. He was not sure what step to take. A family business was at stake, and selling off to a competitor not only meant a family vision was going to be lost, but he would put the lives of many families at risk. When Robert looked in the mirror, he came face to face with the company's logo on a brooch. In that instant it hit him. He realised the principles that the company stood for; principles that had brought them thus far. Robert decided to return the company back to those principles.

Any discussion on the phenomenon of the mirror is incomplete if there was no mention of its most powerful influence: The ability to dictate perception. The mirror is arguably the most potent physical force behind self-esteem.

Sages Elixir

"Whatever the eye sees and the ears hear, the mind believes".

Sage unknown.

Used by many sages throughout the ages.

Like Joanna in the earlier story, our confidence as humans is inextricably linked to how we feel about ourselves. How we feel about ourselves is our self-image. The world sets its standards and the mirror shows us how close we are to those standards. The mirror paints a picture and that picture forms our mental image of ourselves. Nobody, no matter how rich, poor, skilful or clever can run away from their self-esteem. Self-image is so powerful that when it is allowed to become negative, it can lead to disaster, depression and self-harm. When positive self-esteem provides the energy to achieve, it gives a person wings to accomplish feats that were once thought impossible to attain.

Joanna looked in the mirror one day and saw a despondent looking, unattractive lady who would not even chat with a replica of herself. The result was a woman lacking confidence or charm. She was battling with self-image and trying to sell herself at the same time. This is like building a house, and setting it on fire at the same time. Soon she realised like most of us would, that a low self-esteem is perhaps the single most potent destroyer of any human endeavour.

However, the situation changes dramatically when Joanna builds a mental picture of an assured woman. The mirror created this mental picture. It showed her an irresistible woman; an attractive lady whom she would gladly chat with on a 12 hour flight to Melbourne. Suddenly, her confidence was back and she felt like an achiever. With her self-image sorted and her energies now focused on the task at hand, success seemed no longer like a distant dream. In Joanna, we meet one person at two different times. The same person saw two mirror images. The mirror images presented two different mental pictures and in the end, two different results.

Nutshell

Human beings have existed with a natural craving for two things: Knowledge and Relevance. With knowledge comes assurance and with relevance comes happiness. When we look back through history, we are faced with the undeniable truth that our use of mirrors has been key to our successes. Ancient kings have wielded it; religious icons have extolled its qualities; men and women alike have trusted its message; artists have pondered on its power; Scryers have used it for powerful divinations; scientists have employed it at the forefront of their inventions.

Mirrors have brought us vision; the ability to see beyond what our physical eyes can see. Hence it has given us more knowledge. In keeping with the saying that knowledge is power it is not misplaced to say that mirrors have made us more powerful. Mirrors have become a part of our daily routine. In a sense almost all of us rely on mirrors to maintain a positive self-image. Without mirrors we either possess a shaky confidence, or we rely on the previous images they had presented to us sometime in the past.

2 The Seed

Some call it purpose. Some call it destiny or fate. Many call it passion. A few of us prefer to give it a more practical name: The Seed. Whatever name it is called, it points to one thing. Perhaps, it is the answer to one common but intriguing question: Why am I in this world?

It may be a waste of valuable time to engage in the argument of how we found ourselves here on earth. To discuss the merits of the Big Bang or Biblical renditions of creation is outside the scope of this book. Instead, we are concerned with the reality that we are here on earth and what we can make out of being here. I recall sitting in a class where the subject was about food and specifically the prominence of hens in today's dietary needs. Someone went off on a tangent, and asked the contentious question, "What came first, was it the egg or the hen?" A bunch of bored teenagers vehemently tried to argue that the hen existed before the egg and vice versa. In the end, it took close to an hour of endless arguments before we all realised one simple truth: The origin of the hen did not matter half as much as its usefulness.

Like the story of the hen and the egg, everyone has different opinions or beliefs about how we found ourselves here on earth. However, one thing we could all agree on is that making the best use of our lives here is a shared objective. Very many would agree that the times we have felt the most fulfilled in our lives were those times when we did something to aid the life of another person.

Sages Elixir
"Do not ask yourself what the world needs. Ask yourself what makes you come alive. And then go out and do that. Because what the world needs are people who have come alive".

Harold Thurman

Everyone was born with a purpose. This purpose manifests itself in one or both of two ways: Passion or ability. Show me a person without a single passion or ability and I would show you a dead person. In every living thing, there are many abilities. We could start with the abilities that are commonplace and often ignored. There is the ability to talk, think, hear, taste, sing, run, write, juggle, walk, touch, and thousands more. Added to ability is interest. We all have an interest in something. The object of interest could be food, machines,

The Mirror Principle

sports, gadgets, chemicals, music, stories, religion, culture, history, plants, psychology and thousands more.

It is true that we cannot like all objects equally. In the same vein, we are not skilled in the same things equally. In our lives, some things naturally take precedence over others. As we grow up, we start to realise even at an early age that some things come easy to us. We realise that we have the ability to get some things done quicker or more effectively than others. In some cases, other people point this ability out to us. The reason we are usually oblivious to our abilities is that these abilities come naturally to us and we fail to see that others do not have the ability; or where they do they are not as effective as us.

Our lines of interest become obvious over time as well. Even the most dispassionate people have an object that tickles their fancy more than other things in life. In cases where they are unaware of any interests, others around them could point this out to them. I remember once I was a volunteer for a charity event. Young school kids were selected to participate in a charity establishment simulation. In this simulation, the young teens had to choose among themselves a CEO, a fundraiser, an artistic director, an accountant among others. As I stood among the supervisors to observe these kids, it was striking to witness these kids choose among themselves who was best fitted for each role. In less than five minutes, each kid had picked a role and all the roles were taken. It was interesting to see how when one role was called out, all the kids would look in the direction of one particular person. Those glances were acknowledgements of the skill sets that each kid possessed. It reminded us of the truth: Everyone has a natural tendency. It might manifest through ability or interest but it does not hide itself from public glare and acknowledgement.

It is sad to observe how adulthood gradually nibbles away at our passions in life. As children, we are innocent dreamers. As children we see only possibilities and we harbour positive thoughts about doing the things we love. Then we grow a little older and we start to view life as a constant race; a competition against our fellow man. We establish a belief that even for the simplest things in life, only the successes are celebrated; those who fail are mocked and non-participation is most times the safest bet. Then we grow into teenage years when we are constantly reminded that life is not all about us. Or "The world does not revolve around you", as some people might put it. We are reminded that we are just one out of several billions of people on the planet. We grow even older and at this point life is all about meeting certain standards and conforming to society's norms. The next few years of adulthood are spent playing catch up with daily chores, paying bills and learning even more reasons why playing safe is better.

The Mirror Principle

Now our parents desire to make us fend for ourselves is not out of place. Meeting the standards set in society to ensure peace and justice is important. Paying bills is necessary. However, it is the priority we give to these things over our purpose in life that matters. A life completely preoccupied with paying bills or playing catch up with societal trends demonstrates a knack for survival and not a life of true success.

The truth is that everyone is born to be successful at something. There are countless facts that exist to prove this, and some of these facts will be illustrated in this book. Perhaps the strongest allusion to this truth is the mindset of childhood. Childhood is mostly free from the burden of societal conformation. It is in these years, we very clearly harbour our dreams and passions in life. In some cases, our raw skillsets begin to surface, and depending on how much time we give to these skills our areas of strength begin to develop. Even when this passion or purpose goes unattended, it stays buried within us throughout our lifetime; sometimes subdued by societal conformation; many times overshadowed by our fears and doubts.

One of the major extinguishers to our purpose is the mentality that many others can do what we are good at; maybe even better. This notion is one of the greatest distortions of truth on our planet. Yes, someone may be good at doing what you enjoy doing. But they are different from you. They will not do the same thing quite the exact same way as you. People tend to forget that "better" is determined by time as much as by quality. Stay with me as I explain. To say something is better is your estimation of its value. And value itself is derived from demand. Demand changes with time. Therefore demand is transient; meaning that value is transient. With time the value for anything on earth must change. How many times have we seen the thing referred to as "better" yesterday regarded as second best today? And vice versa? Again, what is second best in Europe might be the preferred in Asia. So one may be hailed as "better" than the other, but each one is unique. There are no two human beings exactly alike; no two purposes exactly the same. We might be over seven billion people in the world but everyone has a unique DNA structure, a unique iris pattern and unique fingerprints. Everyone in the world may be brought to one place and made to do a simple task. Everyone will come up with similar results, but each person will put their signature into their result. What you will see if you carefully observe is over seven billion unique works. Everyone has a unique purpose.

Sages Elixir

"To laugh often and much; to win the respect of intelligent people and the affection of children; to earn the appreciation of honest critics and to endure the betrayal of false friends. To appreciate beauty; to find the best in others; to leave the world a bit better whether by a healthy child, a garden patch, or a redeemed social condition; to know that even one life has breathed easier because you have lived. This is to have succeeded."

Ralph Waldo Emerson

Another profound pointer to the uniqueness of purpose is the completeness of the universe. If the natural elements do not balance out each other, then our world would be in chaos; none of us would be able to live in it. The completeness of the universe is a study in perfection. For every night, there is day; for decay there is rebirth; for fire there is water; for the cold winds there is sunshine; plants breathe in carbon dioxide and release oxygen while humans take in the oxygen and release carbon dioxide. Life is like a swinging pendulum; for every move to the right, nature invokes a move to the left.

One fascinating phenomenon is the food chain. The existence of all living organisms is remarkably outlined in a long chain of dependency. From the plankton, which lay beneath the ocean to us human beings, there is a long line of handshakes between thousands of species. Like a conveyor belt of workers, each specie receives from the species before it and passes on to the species next to it. The waste product of one member aids the growth and survival of another.

It is equally fascinating to study the natural workings of the human body. Once a part of the body suffers injury, the body triggers a healing process. Ever had a bruise and forgot about it? Then you checked the spot a few months after and it is as though you were never bruised? Or have you ever been so knackered and riddled with body aches only to go bed for a few hours and wake up feeling fresh and strong. These instances reveal the body's awesome recovery system at work.

There are millions of things that make the world what it is. Many activities give the world its complexity. There is nature, religion, technology, sports, music, art, friendships, the certainty of death, the miracle of life and much more. But just like the human body everything in the universe has a purpose. As the ears hear and eyes see, so do teachers bring us knowledge and doctors keep us in good health. Through science we have begun to realise that virtually no part of the human body is useless. The eyelids for instance, are just a small part of the eye. The eyelid is the thinnest skin on the whole body. But every minute of each day, the eyelids spread tears all

The Mirror Principle

over the eye surface to keep the eyes moist. Is this useful? Absolutely. Without the moisture, the eyes would not function properly. This uncelebrated body part works even while we are asleep. Moreover, this tiny bit of skin performs the vital function called the Blink Reflex. This action protects the eyes from blindness by particles in the air around us. Most times we know nothing about these invasions but the eyelids work diligently to protect one of our most vital gifts: our sight. It is somewhat humbling to realise how many parts of our body go unnoticed but perform functions that keep us alive. So it is with the universe. All things are connected. All things have a unique purpose. Some are more celebrated than others but we must never underestimate the importance of every single thing, event or individual.

Human beings are not left out. We are all dependent on each other. Every man and woman regardless of race, country, age or creed is a unique part of a big picture. Stop for a moment and take a note of how everything around you serves a unique purpose. A map shows you where to go; your clothes keep you warm; your watch tells you the time and your cell phone connects you to people miles away. Everything plays its own part in the big picture. The doctor treats a bus driver using a device just serviced by the software engineer. The engineer used computers that were delivered by the delivery man two weeks ago. The delivery man shops at a local grocery shop which gets its daily stock fresh from a local farmer. The local farmer keenly monitors the daily weather report presented by the weatherman who incidentally depends on the bus driver to get to the office every day. So between these six characters, a circle of dependency is established almost without each party realising how they are connected. In our daily lives, there are millions of these circles of events that link us all together. Even before the advent of the Internet, the world has always been one global village. We are bound together by the web of our endeavours.

All of us inevitably participate in the circle of human connection, but only a few of us realize that we have something inside of us that ultimately enriches the lives of others. I once heard Dr. Myles Munroe say "the richest place in the world is not the oil fields of Iraq, nor is it the gold mines of South America or the diamond mines of South Africa. The richest place in the world is just down the street. It is the cemetery. For there lies companies that were never started, great books that were never written, songs that were never sang, inventions that were never made and masterpieces that were never painted". The cemetery holds millions of square miles of untapped potential. This is sad but true. Many have been trapped by the fear of ridicule. Many have chosen to conform to society's acceptance rather than give life to their innermost dreams. Many fail to realise a profound truth: That happiness is not a function of conformity but a product of giving. Happiness it could be argued is being at peace with the universe. This simply means emptying your gifts to fulfil your part of a universal bargain. In three words: Fulfilling your purpose.

Sages Elixir

"We make a living by what we get but we make a life by what we give".

Winston Churchill

Let us address an age-old question around the subject of purpose. The question is "Are all men born equal?" The answer to this is no. How could all men be born equal? No two persons are born alike. Not even identical twins. Physically they may look the same but we have seen earlier in this chapter that each one is unique. Again, some people are born with many gifts while others are born with few gifts. As we all know, there are people amongst us who were born into this world with disabilities like physical impairment or the inability to see, speak or hear. But the next question should be "Are we all born with gifts?" The answer to this is yes. Even the most disabled child from birth has a purpose in life. As long as you have a soul, you have a purpose.

Your purpose is unique to you, and no one is better than you at what you do. Men tend to compete with others when all they should be doing is competing with their own set goals. If you knew that no one else could be better than you at what you do, the idea of not performing for fear of losing would not come to you. The fact that a child is born in poverty-stricken Somalia does not infer that he or she is not blessed. The fact that a person is born to a certain race, tribe, creed, gender or nation does not automatically mean he or she is disadvantaged. What you may not enjoy in certain aspects of life you often possess an alternative gift that others might not have much of. Remember that just over 60 generations ago, to be a citizen of Rome was perceived as having an advantage over a Native American but that is not the case today. Society always tries to stratify people but it fails to tell us that status is transient. Opportunity is available to all; it simply comes in different forms.

What about those who are born into a poor background? Is coming from a poor or illiterate family a disability? There is a certain disability in poverty or illiteracy but this does not rule out the presence of a seed of purpose. So in that sense, we are all born with certain degrees of disability coupled together with

The Mirror Principle

undeniable abilities. Whether our disability is as conspicuous as a deformed limb or as subtle as an abusive parent, we all still bear a unique purpose, our seed of promise.

Sometimes our disabilities do not surface or exist at birth or childhood. At later stages of our lives we may fall into physical or mental illness or certain degrading circumstances. In spite of this hardship our purpose lies inside of us; waiting to be fulfilled. Disability is all around us but for each man with his hundred disabilities, there is one unique purpose waiting to be unveiled to the world.

It is true that the degree of disability that some people face is so great that it is difficult to sift through the pile of pain and obstacles to unearth the abilities within. To such persons, the highest levels of credit should be reserved. They shall remain in our true Hall of Fame as testaments to the tenacity of the human spirit. Helen Keller was barely a year and half old when she got struck by a brief but severe bout of meningitis. This illness left her deaf and blind for the rest of her life. Helen defied this disability to become the first deaf and blind person to attain a Bachelors of Arts degree. Blessed with a prolific ability in writing, she spent most of her life touching the length and breadth of the world. She wrote over a dozen books and articles; pages that brought succour to many. There is also the story of a certain physicist who started out with a learning disability. He suffered from autism. Some have recorded that he was dumb until the age of three and could not read until he was eight. But this young man concerned himself with his analytical ability. He focused on his strengths. He developed theories that caused breakthroughs in the field of physics. That man was Albert Einstein.

Sages Elixir

"The best and most beautiful things in the world can not be seen or even touched. They must be felt with the heart".

"Many persons have the wrong idea of what constitutes happiness. It is not obtained through self gratification but through fidelity to a worthy purpose".

Helen Keller

Purpose As A Seed

The most striking allegory to human purpose is the seed. All plants come from a seed. Even more importantly, seeds ensure the continuity of life. Every living thing, be it a plant or animal, begins with a seed. A newborn baby was once a sperm. Incidentally a sperm means "seed"; derived from the Greek word "sperma". A giant sequoia tree which grows to as much as 250 feet in height and 25 feet in width started out as a seed barely a quarter of an inch in size. Seeds are one of the most amazing things in the world. In this chapter we will discover the fascinating similarity between seed and purpose.

Some of us can vividly remember our first encounters with a seed. Perhaps it was out in the garden with grandma as she planted those precious fruits and vegetables. Or maybe it was in elementary school while taking part in a science experiment on plants. The first thing that strikes us is that the seeds are so tiny and yet the big plants are contained within. We figure that somewhere within the seed lies a magical ability to grow and blossom into a full-blown plant. We learnt that if you place a seed on a table, it does not grow. But immediately you place the seed on favourable soil and nurture it with some water and sunlight, then the miracle of life unfolds right before your own eyes. In remarkably the same way, when we first discover our purpose or ability, it is useless until we release it. The song is not heard until the singer sings it; the food is not tasted until the one who has the recipe cooks it.

Like a seed, purpose is a life carrying vessel. When purpose comes alive it brings positive energy to those for whom it was intended. In the context of the completeness of the universe, all our individual purposes are connected into one global network. Hence a purpose exists to fill up a void in our world;

just like every seed fills up a void in the food chain in particular and the universe as a whole.

Like a seed, purpose represents the future. The acorns we plant today are the oak trees we shall see in twenty years time. The purpose we discover in ourselves today may hold the keys to our future and perhaps the future of our family, a whole community or an entire nation. Like the blueprint of a skyscraper, purpose is not the end result. Yet purpose is the basic ingredient that spurs the builders into action; the spark that creates the end result. A seed does not always guarantee a plant will emerge in the years or months to come. Rather, it is proof that a plant should exist in the future. Depending on whether the seed is put to use or not, that plant may never exist in the years to come. So too is purpose. It is not a guarantee for accomplishment but rather a proof that the ability resides within us.

Like a seed, purpose is unique. No two purposes are the same. They may be similar but they are never completely the same. This springs from the fact that all human beings are unique. No two persons do the exact same thing the exact same way every time. Every person brings a unique feel to the universe.

The Mirror Principle

FACT

Scientists have discovered techniques to read the DNA of seeds, even those that are labelled as unable to germinate. DNA results reveal that just like humans, each seed possesses a peculiar DNA structure.

Like a seed, untapped purpose stays alive for as long as its host is alive. Untapped potential only dies after the person carrying it has died. Even at the age of a hundred years old or confined to the hospital bed in the latter years of one's life, purpose still resides within its host; waiting to be unleashed to the world. There are many examples of this. Grandma Moses was a remarkable woman. She did not start painting until she was eighty years old. She would go on to complete and sell over seven hundred famous pictures over the next ten years of her life. She worsted wool for embroidered compositions, but was forced to quit due to arthritis. Then in her eighties, she delved into the one thing she had a passion for: painting. In a few years, Grandma Moses had gained renown for her work. One of her paintings was recently valued at 1.2 million USD.

FACT

Israeli archaeologists discovered date palm seeds while excavating in the Desert Mountains of Masada. These seeds were 2000 years old. In 2005, curious scientists planted the seeds and observed it. Records show that these seeds have germinated and blossomed just like any other fresh date palm seed.

Like a seed, tapped purpose lives on after death. Purpose is so powerful that its force can still be felt long after its carrier has passed on. In fact there are cases where a person's purpose although unleashed in his lifetime, is fulfilled long after he is gone. In essence his physical body has decayed as must all human beings but his life lingers on. Such people's lives continue to fill a void in the universe. In other words, purpose can still be fulfilled even after physical death.

The Mirror Principle

FACT

Plant scientists have demonstrated that seeds are capable of reproducing millions of their own type. One well-nurtured seed could survive millions of years as it germinates into a plant that produces more seeds and the process continues. The Puya Raimondi plant also known as Queen of the Andes in South America is known to produce as much as six million seeds in each plant.

At this point, it is helpful to clarify the subtle difference between the life expectancy of a seed and the actual lifetime of a seed. The life expectancy of a seed is the length of time that a seed is expected to last when properly nurtured. Seeds are meant to live for generations. As explained earlier, a seed has the inherent power to multiply into a mighty forest. So even though the actual seed physically decays and disappears from sight, the seed may yet exist in a larger form.

The actual lifetime of a seed is somewhat different. This points to the length of time that the seed actually lived. A seed may have the inherent power to exist for an infinite number of years but may end up living for just a short time. In some cases, the seed does not even get a chance to live at all. Some seeds never get planted, and hence never blossom. Some get planted on the wrong soil, and they fail to grow out of the ground. Some grow into a plant that is harvested but never replanted. There are endless possibilities to how long a seed actually lives for.

This correlates quite well with purpose. There is the life expectancy of a purpose and the actual lifetime of a purpose. The life expectancy of purpose may be infinite. There are some purposes that last through time. This is easily depicted by the lives of those individuals who selflessly gave themselves to a cause; a decision that filled up a void in the universe. Take Einstein for example whose offerings in the field of science have formed the foundations of modern physics, or Mahatma Gandhi whose unflinching struggle continues to form the bedrock for the enterprise of the great nation of India.

The actual lifetime of a purpose implies the length of time that the seed of purpose actually lasted for. Once the physical life of the carrier of purpose ends, the unleashed bubbles of purpose live on. Sadly though, any untapped purpose dies with the carrier.

So like a seed purpose may exist in two forms. One is achievement; where purpose has been tapped and unleashed. The other is potential; where purpose is yet untapped. Very much like a mere unplanted seed or a full-grown tree, purpose could be untapped potential or an achievement. If Grandma Moses had kept on working on embroidery in the last decade of her life, her astonishing paintings would have stayed inside her as untapped potential. Indeed, those paintings would have died with her. The paintings are her gift and they have an infinite life expectancy because they are still alive several hundreds of years on. If she had not ventured into her passion for painting, it is very likely that the actual lifetime of her purpose would have ended when she passed on. The seed would have died with her; purpose would have followed her to the grave.

Sages Elixir

"Though I do not believe that a plant will spring up where no seed has been, I have great faith in a seed. Convince me that you have a seed there, and I am prepared to expect wonders".

Henry D. Thoreau

The Universality of Purpose

Before we move on, it may help to understand another amazing thing about purpose: the universality of purpose. All purposes complement each other to make a perfect universe. One gift balances out the other. What one lacks the other provides. The interdependency of life as we know it precipitates the notion that all gifts are connected in an invisible web of interconnectivity.

There is one aspect of the universality of purpose that is often overlooked. The aspect is that purpose may find its fulfilment in a place very different from where we were born. Most times, we erroneously assume that if our gift is not recognised by those in our immediate circle then it is a waste of time. We tend to forget that there are over seven billion people on the planet. Just in case like me, you struggle to grasp how large seven billion is, you could try and picture it this way: Imagine that you attempted to diligently count seven billion items as quickly as one second at a time. If you started in January 2012, the earliest time you could be through counting will be over two centuries from now in 2235. That is how large seven billion is.

You may be born in Chicago, Illinois in the United States but your purpose may fill a void in Tokyo, Japan. Or you could have grown up in Saudi Arabia but a void in Melbourne, Australia is waiting to be filled by you. Many people allow their immediate environments to limit their dreams. People would argue that a person is confined to their place of birth, country or tribe. But this is a fallacy. In fact more often than not, folks from a different orientation usually seek after our gifts. It is often said that variety is the spice of life. It is true that people tend to appreciate gifts that command some sort of uniqueness.

Your gift might not be the type that thrives in your local community. The onus is on you to take that gift to a place where it meets a need. As a seed flourishes in certain conditions, you have to continually search for a place where your purpose would find natural appeal. To some persons their purpose has a worldwide audience, but to many of us our purpose might find acceptance in a certain industry, country or group of people. The man Jesus lived in Jerusalem just over 2000 years ago. He brought spiritual gifts and relief to many but was greatly underestimated in his local community. He would later go on to make the statement that "a prophet is not recognised in his own house". This phenomenon is understandable, as humans tend to undervalue people they know too well. This is not to say that the ones closest to you are your enemies. Indeed they are your closest allies. They might not be the keenest recipients of your purpose but their support in your life is always valuable.

Does the universality of purpose suggest that you need to travel around the world if the audience to your purpose is on the other side of the planet? The answer is yes and no. Firstly, the answer is no because the world is one global village. Purpose could be deposited in parcels that travel into places that we are not able to physically get to. A gifted singer might not be able to travel around the world but her songs can be heard in all the countries of the world. Secondly, the answer is yes when physical relocation is part of the purpose-fulfilling journey. Things tend to fall into place when physical relocation is necessary for the fulfilment of a purpose. We must remember that purpose has inherent powers of its own. Further pages in this book will show how nurtured purpose finds its audience even when physical relocation is necessary. We will find undeniable proof that nurtured purpose has the inherent power to gravitate towards fulfilment.

Weeds, The Seed's Lifelong Enemy

Seeds grow among weeds. Same way, purpose grows in the midst of many distractions. Modern life is structured in such a way that we are swamped with constant societal expectations. These expectations create a deluge of pressures. For the less financially endowed, a lot of this pressure is centred on money and making ends meet. To the financially endowed, it may be less to do with making ends meet but more to do with coping

The Mirror Principle

with the implications of stupendous wealth. In some cases the pressure stems from parent's expectations, or the emotional burden of making the best use of an inheritance. So every seed has its weeds; every purpose its distractions.

From the young girl born into abject poverty; to the young boy born blind; to the super rich heir to an empire who is struggling with drug addiction; and on to the talented young artist whose parents have enrolled her into law school whilst insisting that she must become a lawyer; there are real challenges everywhere. These challenges like weeds struggle for a place in our lives; they wage a daily war against our seed of purpose. They are real and they are stubborn. The more we prune them out, the more resilient they become. It is like they are constantly saying that they have a pride of place in our lives. Further pages of this book will illustrate how nurtured purpose can succeed in the midst of compelling distractions. We will find profound proof that purpose has the inherent power to outlive the weeds of distraction.

Having pondered on these thoughts, it is somewhat irresistible to ask the question again, "Are some men born more privileged than others?" Before we rush off to an answer, let us bear in mind these three simple truths. Firstly, all men are born with a seed of purpose. Secondly, all men are born with disadvantages regardless of status, country, family fortunes, creed, gender or race. Thirdly, all human beings have a power that no force can take away from them: the power of their uniqueness. Most would agree then that the obvious answer to our question is that "all men are born different but all men have an equal burden to harness their potential".

Nutshell

Passion and Ability: The two key signs to the presence of a seed of purpose. Each one of us is born with a seed of purpose. The uniqueness of every single being, irrespective of age, gender, race or origin lends more credence to the uniqueness of our purpose. In line with the completeness of the universe and the undeniable balance of nature, our unique purposes all come together to give the world its momentum. Together our individual seeds of purpose meet needs in one another's lives in a truly remarkable way. In a sense each of us is a tiny thread that makes up the web of the human network. Some threads may be more visible than others but each thread in the web plays a role in keeping the web balanced and complete.

As the saying goes, "with great power comes great responsibility". We all have the powerful rights to harness our potential. Yet while we recognize these rights we should be loath to forget our responsibilities. The responsibility to fulfil our purpose lies with each of us. Every one of us is faced with that responsibility; the burden of purpose. This burden surfaces in different situations. Our challenge in handling these burdens is made lighter by the fact that purpose has inherent powers that propel it towards its fulfilment. The later chapters of this book will prove this. So despite the disadvantages that we are all born with, we are all gifted with a unique purpose that could help us live a fulfilled life. Neither age nor circumstances of birth can impose a definite barrier to the fulfilment of our purpose.

Purpose stays as potential when untapped. It transcends to achievement when fulfilled. It is only in the fulfilment of purpose that happiness is guaranteed. It is a fair statement to say that the times when we are happiest are the times when we do something we love that meets a need in someone else's life. This is another pointer to the completeness of the human web. There is a natural void in each of us, which is only filled when we meet the needs of others. This shows how much our completeness is tied together. When our purpose comes alive, the world comes alive and our happiness lights up.

The most profound allegory of human purpose is the seed. The essence of human purpose is captured in the life of a seed. A need is proof of the existence of a seed.

3 The Mind

We all marvel at the computer. It is super-fast and intelligent. However there exists a computer that supersedes all known computers by miles. It is all around us. In fact it is within us. It is our body; your body; the human body. Scientists all agree that the human body is an incredibly endowed machine. Remarkably, we live in our bodies but we rarely take the time to understand what we are made of.

It is a good thing to see a growing number of people taking interest in their diet and health. Even more people pay attention to their physical looks ensuring that their bodies are well groomed. Perhaps the least attention is paid to what lies within the body. How does the body work? What does the body consist of? How vast are the internal functions within the body? How do these functions happen?

Our Magical Bodies

The human body is the one thing that we all possess but know the least about. Many people know the outer appearance

The Mirror Principle

of their bodies like they know their names. I know a young aspiring beautician who could glance at a tiny photo and instantly tell you what area of her body that photo shot was taken from. She is trained in the art of physical beauty; she has mastered the features of her outward appearance. She knows every curve, every colour shade, every spot and every mark around her physical body. However as you may have rightly guessed, she knows little about the internal features of her body and how they all work together.

A dedicated study of the inner workings of your body will open some mind-boggling truths to you. According to one medical doctor "it is like walking through the doors of a grandiose estate that has only just been unveiled to you as your inheritance". The body goes beyond hair, eyes, ears, nails and faces. A lot more lies beneath our physical bodies. There are thousands of ads and millions of books that provide us with fantastic advice on how to bring out the best from our outer bodies. Sadly, not as many books throw light on the inner body, and the wealth that lies within it. To exist on earth we all need a body, but the outer body is only kept alive by the functions that go on inside our bodies. To these functions, it is only wise that we pay closer attention.

The body as we know it is a supercomputer with unrivalled ability. Vital organs within the body dictate all our outward actions. It is quite remarkable how the body preserves and protects itself. An undeniable evidence of the body's phenomenal prowess is its ability to heal itself. You might recall cutting up onions or celery, and cutting your fingers in the process; or hitting your foot against the house furniture. When these hurtful incidents occur, nine times out of ten we pamper the cuts or bruises for a little while and then we leave them to heal by themselves. Such is the regenerative power that our body possesses.

Many of us have marvelled at how we tend to wake up at about the same time every morning without the aid of an alarm clock. Scientists have explained that this inbuilt biological clock is part of the "circadian rhythm"; a mental clock that our body sets up by learning our most dominant sleeping habits. How about the fact that we lose close to a hundred strands of hair from our heads each day but the body replaces these hairs within twenty-four hours? Did you realise that your body creates a new skeleton every three months? Or did you know that our body produces a new skin every month? Every second of our lives, ten million cells die and the same number of cells are replaced almost immediately. The body is an amazing thing; perhaps the most potent gift of our lifetime. It is perhaps more capable and more complex than any known thing on the earth.

The Mirror Principle

The Seat of Tremendous Power

At the epicentre of our sophisticated system is the brain; our mental throne room. The brain is an essential part of the central nervous system that controls everything we do. From the complex tasks of building a spacecraft or performing a surgery to acts that are barely noticed like breathing, blinking or swallowing, the brain is constantly working. It is needless to bore you with a biological exposé on the human brain, but what you might gain in the coming pages is an insight into the powerful tool we all carry within us; this magnificent device called the brain.

Often referred to as the soul, the brain and the human mind are one and the same thing. Whether you call it the brain or the mind you would be referring to the seat of human power. Forget the power contained in your arm muscles. The real human power is in the mind. It is within this sublime box that we think, plan and control our actions. Our physical bodies simply do what our mind dictates. Your mind is over a million times more powerful than a million cranes and a million computers put together; the brain can perform a billion more tasks than any man-made object that you can imagine.

A proper scientist may enlighten you with a bit more detail. However, the mind in simple terms is a physical network that consistently sends and receives signals. These signals enable us to live; they help us perform daily tasks from the simplest to the most complex. The mind holds our imagination, emotions, perceptions, ideas, intentions and memory. All these things make us who we are. The mind controls what we do.

Sages Elixir

"The mind is everything. What you think you become."
Buddha

"Mind is the master power that moulds and makes. And we are Mind. And ever more we take the tool of thought and shaping what we will, we bring forth a thousand joys; a thousand ills."
James Allen

This is how the mind works. In our bodies, the brain and the spinal cord make up the central nervous system. This system is a network of nerve cells. These nerve cells are continually sending and receiving millions of electric signals. The signals are our thoughts. As we form thoughts, make decisions, or do even the most basic things, millions of signals are being generated from our nerve cells. These signals are

The Mirror Principle

invisible streams of energy that flow in and out of us. Electrical pulses dispatched by the brain create thoughts.

We could picture the mind as a computer setup. The brain is the physical processor. The nerves are the ports and cables. The energy that powers the computer is our thoughts. Our thoughts are mental energy. It has been proven that the body needs the mind as much as the mind needs the body. This explains why at physical death, a person's thoughts end; mental energy ceases to exist. The physical body starts to decay, as there is no more life to sustain it from within. Likewise if the body is fatally wounded, the flow that sustains the body is broken. It is like pulling the plugs off the computer; the mental energy is cut off.

Perhaps we could illustrate the profound power of the human mind a little more. Some studies show that the human brain contains a hundred billion nerve cells. One nerve cell can produce 1000 pulses per second. The processing power of the average brain is estimated at a hundred million MIPs (Million Information Per second). This is over twenty thousand times more than the fastest computer on earth.

How about memory? One recent study deduced that the biggest computer has the capacity to hold 1012 bytes. Same study shows that the human brain capacity is 108432 bytes. This means that even if we water down the human brain capacity a million times, the gap between the human brain and the most capable computers remains colossal.

FACT

1. The average human brain consists of an estimated one hundred billion nerve cells. They are created in response to mental activity.
2. The brain consists of sixty percent white matter and forty percent grey matter. The nerve cells are contained in the grey matter, and they are responsible for the flow of mental energy. The white matter forms the network on which the mental energy is transported.
3. The brain processing speed can run faster than 120 meters per second. This beats the Ferrari.
4. The brain uses twenty percent of the total energy in the body.
5. The brain uses twenty percent of the total blood in the body.
6. At any point during the day the brain generates between ten and twenty-three watts of power – your brain energy can conveniently power a light bulb.

7. Some experts estimate that the brain produces an average of seven thousand thoughts per day. There are eighty-six thousand four hundred seconds in a day. This implies one thought every 1.2 seconds.
8. Scientists have deduced that the storage capacity of the brain could reach one thousand terabytes. This is impressive when you consider that the National Archives of Britain, which covers over 900 years of history, only takes up 70 terabytes.

The Greatest Computer

Let us remind ourselves of the huge role our mind plays when we perform our daily routines. Some of these routines may seem trivial but the processes running in the background are fascinating. Ever wondered why your toe strikes an object, and in less than a split-second you feel the pain? It is your brain at work. In fact, studies show that the invisible processes within and around us happen at a much faster speed than the actions we take on the outside. Indeed the invisible is more powerful than the visible.

The human vision is one of such amazing things. Do you know what happens when you watch television? How much work the mind is doing? The eye and the brain can distinguish between 10 million colours. For every second you look at the TV, the mind performs complex calculations. The eye uses six main muscles to move in different directions. It picks up the signals from the TV in the form of light. The light passes through the cornea to the retina that sits behind the eye. The retina contains photoreceptors that our humorous opticians fondly call the rods and cones. These cells are made up of a photosensitive chemical called Rhodopsin. Within a millionth of a second the incoming light activates this chemical; creating electrical impulses in the process. These impulses send super-fast signals to the brain. The brain then uses different clusters of cells to perform the most sophisticated image recognition process. All of this is done within a fraction of a second. We process millions of this vision-processing-activity on any given day as long as our eyes are open.

How about when you are walking barefoot around the house? For every step you take, the brain is continually processing the signals from your feet. The skin all over our bodies contains tiny nerve endings called receptors. These receptors feed the brain with information about anything your body comes in contact with. The body is so sophisticated that it has different types of receptors that tell the brain more about the surface your feet are touching. Amongst others you have heat, cold, pain and pressure receptors. Within a fraction of a

The Mirror Principle

second, these receptors help you to know how hot, cold, painful or smooth the floor is.

Most times, all these receptors are working at the same time. For every single step you take, electrical signals are sent through the spinal cord to the brain. The brain determines the feeling from the type of signal. Then it decides if any course of action is required to maintain the feet's state of health. If in this case you have stepped upon a sharp object that pierces your skin, the brain receives signals from the pain receptors. Then it acts by sending signals to specific hormones in the body that release chemicals that have an analgesic effect; an effect that can stop or reduce pain sensations. Suffice to say that all of these signals travel back and forth within a fraction of a second.

Research reveals that we blink our eyes on an average of twenty thousand times a day. Each time we blink, the brain works to keep things illuminated so that the whole world around us does not go dark. Blinking itself is a reflex action that moisturises the eyes with tears and protects the eye from foreign invasion.

Ever wondered why you shiver in a cold place? Shivering is your body's automatic response to temperatures colder than the normal body temperature. As receptors on your skin sense an undesirable drop in body heat, signals are sent to the brain, which in turn sends signals to muscle groups around vital organs. These muscle groups begin to shake in small movements to create body heat. Hence you shiver, and even without being conscious of it your body is increasing its own heat. On the flip side we have sweating. As you experience heat, your body produces water through the skin pores to cool you down.

Thoughts – Those Mighty Things

All of these things could make you wonder, "What does the mind use to make these decisions? How does the mind know the right decisions to make? How many of these decisions am I in control of?"

This brings us to some more interesting facts about the mind. Earlier we mentioned that the mind sends and receives signals to achieve anything it does. These signals are familiar to you. They are called thoughts. Like most things in the world, thoughts exist in different forms. Memory, emotions, willpower, beliefs, reasoning, perception and imagination are different forms of thought. Thought is the fundamental unit of the mind. As an ocean is made of little drops of water and the desert is a collection of tiny sand particles, so is the mind a pool of thoughts. Let us take a closer look at the mind and how it is set up.

The Conscious and the Subconscious

Centuries of research have adduced that the mind can be divided into two distinct parts: The conscious and the subconscious. Both are powerful in their own right and they work hand in hand. The conscious mind is at work when we deliberately do something. The subconscious mind is at work when we do something that we are not entirely aware of. The conscious mind is the foremost part of the mind where we perform logical reasoning and make decisions. It is the seat of willpower and reasoning. The subconscious is a much larger part of the mind that seats behind the conscious mind. In fact some scientists tend to discard the use of the term "sub" to avoid wrong interpretations that the subconscious is a part of the conscious. It is actually termed "sub" because of its location. The subconscious is located in the deep recesses of our minds. It is the seat of our emotions, memory, beliefs, perception and imagination. It is such a powerful part of our minds that it goes into action once our conscious mind switches off. Even when our conscious mind is at work, the subconscious is very busy controlling many things that we are seldom aware of.

Picture this. When you are shopping for groceries and you reach out for a certain item on the shelf; that is your conscious mind at work. It reasons, it decides and then you act. Yet at that very point, your subconscious was even busier. You were breathing but you were not aware. You were slightly bent over to take a closer look at the item on the shelf but you were not aware. Your feet were rooted to the floor to keep you balanced but you were not aware. That was your subconscious at work. Even when we sleep, and our conscious mind switches off, the subconscious is at work using our imagination to create dreams.

One easy way to show the difference between the conscious and the subconscious minds is by monitoring your breathing. Make a deliberate effort to control your breathing. When you do this, your conscious mind is at work; the pace of your breathing is intentional. Once you stop focusing on your breathing and you get on with other things, it is your subconscious that takes over the breathing process.

The conscious mind rationalizes things and decides what we do. It is almost impossible to rationalize all the actions we take every passing second. Imagine the chaos that would occur if every second, you had to decide how to breathe, where you are, when you should blink, make sense of the words on the newspaper in front of you and figure out the temperature of the room you are in. Astonishingly we do all these and much more within a second. However, we are only aware of the words on the newspaper. Our conscious mind can only process one line of thought in a single moment. Well on a lighter note, considering that women are excellent at multitasking, the statistic might be even lower for most men.

So how do we perform all these actions in a matter of seconds? This is where the subconscious mind comes into play. The subconscious is a doer. It does not evaluate or rationalize. It just does. It is like a large pre-programmed alarm system that goes off in response to prevailing conditions. Next time you yawn, remember that it is simply your subconscious realising that your brain is short on oxygen hence the intake of air. Your subconscious does thousands of things on your behalf every second of your day.

Unlike the conscious mind, the subconscious decides our actions based on past information and patterns. It receives instructions from our conscious mind, and forms a thick wall of beliefs and emotions. When the conscious mind is too busy with immediate thought, the subconscious uses these beliefs to make decisions that cause us to act. Our conscious mind uses repetition to impress character on our subconscious. As we learn new things or believe any notion, the conscious mind hands the thought over to our subconscious. The subconscious is so sophisticated that it weighs the thought and works out what part of our memory it should reside. This is why the emotion with which a thought is received in the conscious mind is very important.

Facts show that our subconscious is like a large storage room. It is complex but extremely well organised. It has different compartments for different forms of thought. Emotions could be stacked at one end while beliefs are stacked at another. Thoughts are stored like for like. For example, the thoughts responsible for our beliefs are aligned based on the type of emotions they are related to. Psychologists say the reason the subconscious does this alignment is that it uses the principle of association to provide answers. After an experience, the subconscious builds a layer of information by associating one thought with existing ones. It links new thoughts to old thoughts with which it finds a relationship.

This is the reason we can recall things quicker when they are associated with a certain smell. I cannot quite count the number of past events that had suddenly popped into my head, as I smelt a certain fragrance. Or the memories I thought were lost which flashed back so clearly when a certain song came on the airwaves. That is the power of the subconscious. What happened was that my subconscious had picked up the smell or sounds when it recorded the event. It then linked the thoughts of the smell or sound with the memory of the event. So when that smell or sound showed up several years later, the subconscious flooded my conscious mind with the event. How many times have you listened to a playlist often enough that your mind plays the next soundtrack to you before it actually begins?

Sages Elixir

"The conscious mind may be compared to a fountain playing in the sun and falling back into the great subterranean pool of subconscious mind from which it rises."

Sigmund Freud

The way the subconscious operates can work for or against our good. The subconscious believes that whatever we have fed to it is there for our good. It is so powerful that it loses nothing throughout our lifetime. It has every single thing well stored in the order in which we have received these thoughts. Although our subconscious started out as a clean slate, every course of action we take has been learned and added on to that slate. Hence we are able to do things involuntarily. Only when we reason, do we do things with the conscious mind. At other times, the subconscious works on our behalf and takes control.

I once read the story of Mr. Rogers, a forty-year-old man who suffered from one of the strangest phobias in the world.

He had Anthophobia; the fear of flowers. It was so bad that Rogers could not pass within three metres of any kind of flower. An accidental entrance into a room adorned with flowers would cause the most frantic of screams and trauma. After months of undergoing therapy, his therapist discovered the cause of this disorder, and Rogers was able to overcome this embarrassing fear. "But who could be afraid of flowers?" you might ask with wonder, but this can happen to anybody.

It so happened that when Rogers was just four, he had gone into the woods to play. On discovering a beautiful scene of flowers amongst the bushes, he decided to reach closer and smell them. Unknown to him, he had disturbed a hive of very dangerous bees. Within seconds the bees were all over him, stinging him all over; a thousand agonising stings to the face and neck. He did not even have enough time to use his hands to cover his face. He attests that he never saw the bees. All he heard was the humming of a thousand bees. Doctors said it was a miracle that Rogers survived. His face was slightly damaged. After this experience, the man could never see a bunch of flowers without experiencing trauma.

What happened in Rogers' case is that from this near-death experience, his subconscious had related flowers to the feelings of anxiety and untold fear. The subconscious knows no better. Remember, it operates by the principle of association. It does

The Mirror Principle

not know good or bad; it links one perception or memory to another. So in the mind of Rogers, flowers brought unspeakable horror. Even though we all know that flowers are nice, harmless things of beauty, the strongest link that Rogers had to flowers were emotions of pain and distress. It was only after dedicated sessions with a trained therapist that Rogers was able to convince his subconscious that flowers were not harmful.

Unlike Rogers, many of us do not have life threatening phobias. However, like Rogers, all of us have fears and anxieties. These feelings are understandably tied to past experiences. Sometimes our conscious mind does not even remember why we fear the things we fear, but they are already stored down there in our subconscious. Maybe it was something we heard, or saw, or felt. Some of us fear darkness, heights, spiders, or other insects. These fears are a product of past experiences. Remember that for anything you experience, the subconscious takes notes, and reproduces these notes when it meets a similar experience in the future.

The Auto Pilot

Your mind is very similar to a pilot on an aircraft. The aircraft typifies your life. The pilot is your mind. The huge flying object which is your life is being controlled by one little fellow; your mind the pilot. Just like the pilot, your mind pushes buttons to dictate the direction, altitude and speed of the aircraft. So what happens when the pilot needs to attend to something else besides flying the aircraft? The answer is simple. The pilot switches to Auto Pilot. At this point the pilot is no longer controlling the aircraft. It is being controlled by a programmed system. In this illustration, the conscious mind is the pilot; the subconscious is the autopilot. The autopilot is so sophisticated that it performs more checks and actions than the pilot.

Such is the workings of the conscious mind and the subconscious. Remember when you first learned to ride a bicycle or drive a car? For the first few days, you are unable to ride or drive and narrate a story at the same time. This is because you need to stay focused, and you need to think through the action you are taking. At this point you are using your conscious mind. However, after several years of riding or driving, you can conveniently ride or drive while narrating a story to someone else. What has happened is that the driving has become a natural habit, and you do not need to think to do it. That skill has moved on to autopilot mode. The subconscious has taken over. If you have ever had difficulties with typing on a computer keyboard like I did, you would probably remember how slow you were when you first attempted to type. But with constant practice, you get on the keyboard and your fingers just seem to know where every letter is on the keyboard.

Habits

This is where habits become very important in our lives. Habits are a direct result of repetition. Through repetition of any action, the subconscious acts on its own to perform that action anytime it reckons that action is needed. It has been trained by our previous thoughts and actions; right from the inception of our lives. Habits are so strong that we do not need to be aware of them when we engage in them. As water takes the shape of its container, so does the mind take the shape of our habits.

Sages Elixir

"Habit is based on the principle that all things are created twice. There is a mental creation and then there is a physical creation. The physical creation follows the mental just as a building follows its blueprint"

Stephen R. Covey

In the 21st century we tend to refer to habit as though it is a negative thing. Habits are not always negative practices that we need to get rid of. Far from it; habits could be good or bad. Like a fire, habits could either hurt us or serve us. The choice is entirely up to us and the kind of habits we train ourselves to have.

The training to form a habit usually finds its difficult moments only at the onset. Depending on how much resistance our subconscious applies to it at the start, habits take some time to form. As long as our conscious continually engages in a certain line of thought, a habit is guaranteed. And when habits are formed, like red wine on a silk dress, they take their place in our lives. It is amazing how a skill we tried so hard to perfect, when it takes root, is harder still to unlearn. First we form habits, and then they turn around to form us.

Sages Elixir

"Sow a thought and you reap an action; sow an action and you reap a habit; sow a habit and you reap a character; sow a character and you reap a destiny"

Ralph Waldo Emerson

I once listened to a psychologist whose simple explanation made a lot of sense. A mother had complained about her child's intentional absence from school any time she was working out of town. The psychologist opined that the child's habits were in the way. She said habits involve a stimulus and a response. The indolent child goes to school not as a response to any stimulus in the school itself, but as a response to the pressure of his mother's will. When that stimulus is absent, the response does not occur. Hence the child happily stays away from school.

Indeed all our reactions are linked to our beliefs and emotions. We are constantly reacting to things. Our lives are like the moving hands of a clock. Already programmed to act a certain way, we press on towards a certain direction every passing second. We are creatures of habit. The only time we stop reacting and start acting is when we use our conscious minds to make new decisions or learn something new. We cannot use our conscious minds all the time; therefore we are truly at the mercy of the thoughts formed in the subconscious mind. This is the reason why one person would run away from a dog, and another would run towards it. It is the same object but different reactions simply because of different beliefs. This is why one person would see success as achievable and another sees it as unattainable. For the former it is close; for the latter it is too far away. Different habits of thought see the same thing but produce opposite reactions.

Some Masters of the Mind

Many people treat the act of hypnosis with suspicion. It is easy to see why they remain sceptical when you consider the number of times innocent people have been manipulated by self-helping hypnotists. These hypnotists use their knowledge of the subconscious to outsmart unsuspecting victims. However on the positive side, hypnosis is an interesting revelation to how habits are formed. The major weapon used by hypnotists is repetition. By continually repeating a certain image or sound and associating that image or sound with a particular notion, a person's mind takes on that notion. Hence there are thousands of Japanese Taoists and Buddhist monks who can walk barefoot over a bed of red-hot coal without feeling pain. These are pointers to the power of the human mind.

Have you ever wondered why it is that you like a certain thing so much even though there are other varieties or brands of the same thing in existence? The reason is simple. Our mind is a sophisticated machine that associates all things with a particular belief or emotion. Hence at any point in time even without rationalizing in our conscious minds, it is the object that invokes our strongest emotion that wins. Advertising experts have perfected this art; the art of linking commercial

The Mirror Principle

products to the stronger feelings within us. This is why products are subtly associated with images that we adore. There was Pepsi and a certain Michael Jackson, Coca-Cola and football legends, and skin products and famous Hollywood stars. Advertisers believe that once they can register your love for a certain figure with their product, chances are that you inexplicably link that bias to their product. And this works.

It is all about striking the right emotional chords within us; reactions merely follow. I know of countless times I have embraced a particular product amongst many alternatives only because a person I looked up to was associated with it. In some cases it was only a soundtrack associated with the advert. It was not my favourite product, but I responded to my favourite song and hence the product. Sometimes the things that invoke the strongest emotions from us are things for which we have no logical explanation why we like them. The objects of our deepest associations go beyond logical explanations. Experts call these objects Lovemarks. They are objects we love beyond the realms of reason. Some have said that this is the deepest form of attraction; a love for something that cannot be rationalized. For some, one of their lovemarks is the smell of coffee; for some it is a particular colour; for some it is a certain event; for others it is a particular person.

So we have shared much about the mind and how it works. To end this chapter, we shall share another astonishing discovery. The next few pages are dedicated to the profound revelation of how the mind relates with the universe.

The Timeless Connection Between The Mind and The Universe

On earlier pages we touched on two key truths. The first was the oneness of the universe. We understood that all things that exist complement each other. When one thing fails to fulfil its purpose it leaves a void in the universe. This causes an imbalance that the universe works frantically to correct. The second truth was that thought is the basic unit of the mind. What we know as the mind is actually mental energy, and the basic unit of mental energy is thought. Thoughts have several forms. Emotions, ideas, knowledge, beliefs, skills, imagination and memory are all different forms of thought.

If thought is the basic unit of the mind, what then are thoughts? A thought is simply an electrical signal produced by neurons that make up the nervous system. When your brain is at work, it has billions of neurons sending out signals. These signals are thoughts; they form the basis of the actions we take and everything we know. Both the conscious and the subconscious minds utilize thoughts to circulate information and cause action.

FACT

1. Scientists have proven for over hundreds of years now that thoughts are created by neural electrical impulses dispatched by the mind.
2. Science has proven that the time taken between the birth of a thought and the physical action as a result of that thought takes only as little as one millionth of a second. An average person is capable of consciously releasing as much as one million units of mental energy per second.
3. Lines of thought are often confused to be the same as thoughts. The human mind is capable of 70,000 lines of thought per day but produces over one billion thoughts or mental signals every day.

Science has begun to give credence to the fact that thoughts are signals, and hence they are a form of matter. Thoughts carry mental energy. We cannot see air, but it is matter and it is all around us. We cannot see thoughts with our naked eyes, but they are powerful energy carrying matter. Just as telephone signals are invisible masses of matter so too are our thoughts.

We may not see these signals, but they are real and we can feel them.

Several years ago, the BBC reported that scientists in the MCP Hahnemann University School of Medicine in Philadelphia, United States demonstrated that brain cell activities could actually be used to control a robotic device. Rats were trained to control a robotic arm by pressing on a lever. During this training, scientists recorded the brain signals that were associated with these movements. Soon they took off the lever and with the use of electrodes attached to the rat they connected a robotic arm to the rat's brain activity. The rats initially found some difficulty with life without the physical lever. With time they adapted to this new kind of control, and they discovered just like the watching scientists that the brain activity alone was sufficient to move a robotic object. The only other challenge the scientists faced was establishing a more subtle connectivity between the brain and the object.

One of the simple facts that we learn in elementary school is that all things exist as matter. Matter is simply anything that has weight and occupies space. Later on we were taught that even particles that are invisible to the naked eye are kinds of matter. We know for a fact that all the objects we see, whether large or small, are made up of tiny particles. If you go beyond the surface and see things for what they basically are you would

The Mirror Principle

see that all things are composed of matter. Matter is the basic underlying thing.

Matter is a continuous movement of particles, which are held together by the forces of attraction. Hence right inside that table in front of you, though it may look solid and stationery, there are thousands of mobile particles within it; held together by the forces of attraction. Again at school, we were rightly taught that these particles are constantly vibrating. Even though the table looks solid it is vibrating inside. In fact all things consist of vibrating particles. Let us take the three states of water for example. Ice, water and vapour all contain vibrating particles. The only difference between these three states of water is that the vibrating particles are packed with different levels of tightness. Solid ice retains a fixed shape because its vibrating particles are locked into place. Liquid water assumes the shape of its container because its vibrating particles are less compact. The gaseous steam however, assumes the shape of its container but its vibrating particles are so loosely held that they can flow in several directions. Such is the essence of matter.

The mind is a container of thoughts. These thoughts are particles with electrical charges. Hence thoughts attract and repel other thoughts. The universe is a complete mass of matter and the mind is a part of that conundrum. As the mind continually sends and receives signals, it is a part of the interaction of matter that makes the universe what it is. According to quantum physics, all physical reality is made up of vibrations of energy. This includes literarily everything you can think of. Objects, sounds, light, walls, thoughts, clothes, pens, chairs; the whole lot. Each one carries vibrating particles. They interact by the forces of attraction which all particles release. It is all these interactions that make our universe what it is.

The universe is an immense web of dynamic energy. The universe as we know it is a quantum sea filled with vibrating energy. When you study the conclusions of people who have had the rare opportunity to study our universe, you will find a common thread of revelation. This thread is the undeniable fact that all things that exist are connected together by an intricate web of energy. Edgar Mitchell was an astronaut on Apollo 14. On a three-day journey back to earth on the Apollo 14, he witnessed earth from space. In his words "the presence of divinity became almost palpable, and I knew that life in the universe was not just an accident based on random processes. I was engulfed by a sense of universal connectedness; the knowledge came to me directly". He was only the sixth human to walk on the moon. Edgar founded the Noetic Institute of

The Mirror Principle

Science in 1973. The society's motto is to encourage and conduct research on human potential.

I pause at this juncture to point out something simple yet powerful. The fact that you do not see the connectedness of matter around you does not mean it does not exist. I for one tend to have an "I will believe it when I see it" kind of disposition. However, that notion changed when I was confronted with a simple illustration, and here it goes: If a car was to speed past you at say a hundred miles per hour you will see it race past you; in other words, it has just raced past you, and it is there; it exists. If the same car was made to accelerate even faster, you will only catch glimpses of it as it races past. Accelerate even more, and you will catch slighter and slighter glimpses for each time the speed is increased. Yet, the car still exists. Now let us introduce a tremendously high amount of speed, to the degree that your naked eyes cannot catch it speed past you. The car has sped past you at such a high speed that your naked eyes cannot grasp it. Yet, the car still exists. In essence the car has sped at a frequency beyond the reach of your physical eyes. The car exists; the event of the car speeding past you happened; you just did not see it with your naked eyes because the event happened at a frequency beyond what your physical eyes could grasp. In similar fashion, our thoughts and all forms of matter within the universe all strive towards maintaining a balance within the universe. It is happening; we just do not see it.

Even the processes in our body show that all things yearn for balance. Indeed the entire universe yearns for balance. In a way, all things living and non-living exist to ensure the continuity of the universal balance. Any unfulfilled potential; any thoughtless consumption; any injury to the human body causes an imbalance that reverberates all through the universe.

Resonance is the Key

Have you ever heard of resonance? The physics of resonance is simple but powerful. Resonance occurs when two vibrating objects affect each other by sharing the same vibrating frequency. Rather than bore you with scientific jargon, let us use everyday events to demonstrate the law of resonance.

Have you ever sat in a room when a heavy truck roared past on the street nearby? Then as if playing out its role from a script the chandeliers responded with a clattering sound? Or the steel spoon on the dinner table shakes even though everything else remained unmoved? Again, I was amazed to see the same phenomenon demonstrated by an opera singer. She broke a wine glass several metres away simply by singing in a very high-pitched voice. All she did was galvanise her voice into a piercing loud cry. As she kept belting out this high pitch, the thin glass first cracked and then shattered into two parts within seconds. At the time, I looked around me. I seemed to be the only shocked person in the audience. Apparently, the others had seen her perform this act countless times. And perhaps, they understood a concept which I had only just begun to learn; the law of resonance. When two things are vibrating at the same frequency, the forces of attraction are initiated, and one of these two things must affect the other.

The stationary object was vibrating at a particular frequency. The moving truck or the high-pitched sound from the opera singer gained the same frequency as the stationary object. They attracted and interacted with the object, which caused a reaction from the object.

There is also the example of the narrow bridge at Tacoma, Washington. First built in 1940, the bridge began to vibrate excessively even without any mechanical faults. After four months, the bridge collapsed. Some experts say that the wind had caused the bridge to resonate. The bridge was designed to resist strong winds of up to 120 miles per hour, but a wind of 42 miles per hour operated at a frequency that matched the structural frequency of the bridge and hence the bridge gave way. Modern civil engineers take serious heed to the law of resonance.

Sages Elixir

"All matter originates and exists only by virtue of a force. We must assume that behind this force lies the existence of a conscious and intelligent mind. This mind is the matrix of all matter"

Max Planck

"Everything in the universe has a rhythm. Everything dances"

Maya Angelou

So it is true; our minds are like radio transmitters. Our mental energy depicts the radio waves we produce. Our nerve cells are producing and receiving these powerful radio waves. Just like a radio transmitter, our mind operates by the law of resonance. We receive things based on the frequency that our thoughts are tuned into; we send signals based on the frequency of our most dominant thoughts.

Another interesting fact we hinted at earlier is that thoughts come in different forms. Hence each thought operates at a certain frequency. For instance, the frequency at which the

The Mirror Principle

emotion of love operates is very different from the frequency for the emotion of fear. Our mind works brilliantly at storing the different thoughts in different compartments. Like a library, the mind is divided into several sections. Each section represents a distinct form of thought. Just like a library stores books according to the various disciplines and then groups these books by specific subjects, the mind stores thoughts in different compartments and arranges similar thoughts together. If you walked into a well organised library, you would find that the books have been archived into several compartments. There could be a science section. Within the science section, books may again be arranged into subsections like agricultural science, animal science, soil science, chemistry, physics and many more. Again within the physics subsection, books could be arranged into more subsections like quantum physics, optical physics, atomic physics and many more. And the stratification continues to the last book. The mind acts in a similar way; storing our thoughts by associating them; linking similar thoughts together. This sophisticated storage system is founded on resonance. Thoughts of similar frequency attract each other, and they are stored together.

FACT

1. Authenticated research has proven that humans continually create new neurons (thought producing cells) throughout life. The interesting bit is that neurons are created in response to mental activity.
2. Studies have shown that the brain tissues responsible for our thoughts continue to grow throughout our lifetime.
3. A small area of the brain called Amygdala is responsible for your ability to read people's facial expressions and discern if they are angry, happy, surprised or sad.

Interestingly, in the field of advanced medicine there is a common knowledge. Neurons, the cells responsible for thoughts are produced in direct proportion to our mental activity. This is referred to as Neuroplasticity or Brain Plasticity. In simple terms, our brain cells can increase without limit; the only limitation to this increase is how much we use the brain. There are many examples to prove this.

Before we look at some irrefutable examples, it is about time we mention and try to address one of the world's most famous arguments. It stems from a simple statement, quoted by some intelligent minds and used unsparingly in many promotions. It is the "ten percent myth"; the saying that we only use about ten percent of our brains. Is this true or false?

The Mental Gym

We all know now through brain scans that when we suffer illnesses like Parkinson's disease or stroke induced ailments; a sizeable part of our brain is damaged. Doctors show that as much as sixty percent damage to the brain could render a sufferer handicapped. To then say that ninety percent of our brain is unused would mean that we would be unable to perform even the most basic of functions. All of our brain is in use at one time or the other to perform the basic human functions. So it is a false notion to infer that we only use ten percent of our brains.

However, it gets even more interesting. What is true is that we only use less than ten percent of the potential of the human brain. The brain does not have muscles but consists of tissues that can expand. These tissues interact with the outside world using signals called thoughts. Like muscles, the brain regions can expand through practice. Studies have shown that through practice of a particular line of thought, parts of the brain expand.

Albert Einstein is regarded as a genius. His physical brain has been the subject of much study. Verified findings show that the brain of Einstein was similar in size to the brain of the average human being. In the region that is responsible for mathematics and spatial perception, that part of his brain was 30 percent wider than the average. The reason is obvious. Through sustained practice in mathematics and physics, that area of Einstein's brain expanded. Just as our physical muscles can be developed through exercise, so can the regions of our brain be developed. Through mental exercise we develop areas of our brain where the thoughts related to such exercises are resident.

FACT

The famous London taxi drivers are renowned for knowing all the streets of London by name and location. Scans have shown that the hippocampus, the part of the brain responsible for memory and spatial navigation, of these drivers was larger than that of other people. In this study, the hippocampus increased in direct proportion to the length of time the taxi driver had been on the job.

The Mirror Principle

This is the key reason why blind people are renowned for having a better ability to locate the direction of sound than other people. Through the constant use of echolocation, which is the act of locating the source of sound, they have trained the hearing functions of their brain much better than those who can see.

Sages Elixir

"The mind once exposed to the dimensions of larger ideas never returns to its original size"

Oliver W. Holmes

Researchers performed a study on mice. A set of mice was kept in one cage that was furnished with toys and gadgets. Another set of mice was kept in a bare cage. Both sets of mice had brain scans before and after the period of the experiment. At the end of the experiment, it was revealed that the mice that had been surrounded with the toys and gadgets had grown far more dendrites in their brains. The other set that lived in the bare cage had little or no brain changes. Dendrites are the part of the brain upon which thought signals travel. The mice aided with toys had experienced more brain activity and released more signals than the other set of mice. The obvious conclusion of this study is that the brain develops through training.

No Limits On This Machine

Ever wondered why there were certain unbelievable feats that you achieved at a time you were under great pressure; feats you could not have achieved in your normal state? Well, I remember a few. One of them occurred when I was thirteen years old. At the time, I had a fear for the vicious looking dogs called Alsatians. I remember paying a visit to a neighbour's home and for some reason their Alsatian was always in a bad mood; or maybe it was just the effect I had on the dog. On this day my neighbours were out, and had left the dog by itself in the house. As I found my way into their backyard I sensed a force of rage coming from behind me. I turned to find the Alsatian speeding towards me as though it was going to tear me to shreds. Instinctively I ran for my dear life. But I was not running fast enough. It was a fairly large compound. The dog was closing in; fuelled by my fear and screams. I knew I had just one choice; jump over the eight-foot fence for safety. On a normal day, I would not be able to lift myself over a five-foot fence. But on this day, without any previous training and aided only by the instinct to survive, I lifted myself. As though assisted by some powerful wings, I jumped over the fence, and landed on the other side to safety. That incident felt like a miracle of some sorts. When I went back to the spot several days after, I could not fathom how I achieved such a feat.

Now, having gained more insight into human potential, I understand what occurred. I was propelled by a power unleashed by my brain; a power we all have within our bodies; a power controlled by the mind. The invisible wing that I felt lift me up on that day is a substance called adrenaline. I had achieved a feat beyond my normal abilities; yet the power to achieve that feat was always within me. All I needed was a pressured situation, and the ability within me was stirred.

This is how adrenaline works. When we are faced with a dangerous situation and want to survive, a part of the brain is stimulated. This part of the brain is called the hypothalamus. It sends out thought signals to your adrenal glands that bring your sympathetic system into life. This system has mind-blowing tendencies. The sympathetic system is responsible for sending your entire body into an excited state. The adrenal hormones allow the muscles to contract beyond normal limits. This allows blood and oxygen to flow into your muscles at a heightened rate. In this state, we are capable of tremendous feats; we can be far more agile, process information quicker and use up more energy. This is why a woman could lift a two thousand pound object at the sight of her son pinned underneath a car.

Biologists are still trying to determine how long we can sustain such excited states without causing injury to ourselves. Hence it is very possible that no human can live every moment of their lives in such states without doing harm to their bodies. The actual lesson here is not for us to seek to be in this state for twenty hours of the day; the lesson is for us to be aware that the mind can expand to an almost infinite capacity. Our mind should be used more as a springboard rather than a restriction. Given the right stimulation humans are capable of tremendous feats; it all begins with the mind.

Sages Elixir

"The empires of the future are the empires of the mind"
Winston Churchill

"Empires would fall; dynasties would fade away but the mind of man will survive the destruction of all inanimate matter. Its destiny is internal"
Edward Counsel

The Mirror Principle

"There are no constraints on the human mind; no walls around the human spirit; no barriers to our progress except those which we ourselves erect"

Ronald Reagan

"As your habitual thoughts are, so also would be the character of your mind; for your mind is dyed by the colour of your thoughts"

Marcus Aurelius

"It is the mind that makes good or ill; that makes wretched or happy; rich or poor"

Edmund Spenser

This leads us to conclude that there is no such thing as luck. Many might yet argue that many things happen outside of our control. This is true, but what is also true is that all things are a result of a sequence of events. Nothing really happens out of the blue. We are actually in control of as much as we want to be in control of. Such is the freedom associated with the human enterprise. Even the use of medication to enhance our performance points to the same fact: There is unused potential present in our most powerful asset; The Mind.

FACT

1. Brain enhancing drugs like Omega-3 contain Docosahexaenoic acid (DHA) that makes the cell membranes more elastic. Cell membranes are masses of fat that connect the brain cells together. They transport the brain signals. Hence when DHA is administered to the brain, the thought signals travel faster between the brain cells.
2. The mind is so powerful that doctors attest that up to 65 percent of their patients suffer physical ailments that could be traced to psychological reasons.

Nutshell

Charles C. Colton's statement sums up this chapter. He said "There is an elasticity in the human mind capable of bearing much, but which will not show itself until a certain weight of affliction is put upon it. Its powers may be compared to those vehicles whose springs are so contrived that they get on smoothly when loaded; but jolt confoundedly when they have nothing to bear". "Tyrants", Caleb remarked, "have not yet discovered any chains that can fetter the mind".

We have learned that our minds consist of two powerful parts. There is the conscious mind that acts as a gatekeeper and regulates what we believe. It rationalizes and makes us act. Then there is the subconscious mind that many including me believe is even more powerful. It works a million times faster than our conscious mind; it is at work even when we are asleep.

The subconscious works through suggestion and repetition from the conscious. Whatever thoughts our conscious mind receives continually it impresses on our subconscious, and it becomes an established belief. It is similar to a pathway created in the woods. Through constant treading of feet along a particular path, a pathway is created. The subconscious makes a mental pathway from thoughts that dominate our lives. Furthermore, as though this was not sophisticated enough, the subconscious organizes these thoughts into different compartments. It relates similar emotions and memories together and links them up to our perceptions; hence the power that our favourite music and other indulgences exert upon us.

The universe is a collection of matter. Thoughts are a form of matter. Therefore our minds connect with the universe.

There is also the phenomenon called resonance; the law that makes all matter that vibrate at the same frequency to experience a force of attraction. Hence our thoughts are ever so capable of connecting to other forms of matter around the universe. What is more, the mind's creative ability is infinite. The mind is capable of thinking beyond whatever it has previously thought of or accomplished. Our mind is a potent force.

4 Mirror Principle: The Seed, The Mirror and The Mind

All we have talked about thus far; everything we have said; all the facts we have discussed were meant to bring us here. At this juncture we stand face to face with a timeless law; a law that strikes at the very heart of any significant human endeavour. We are talking about a law so powerful that it can turn a bundle of misery into a spectacle of success, and any human achievement into a specimen in disaster. This law has existed since the beginning of mankind. Through time it has been the chief cornerstone of all known failures and successes. The law transcends all industries, continents, race, gender or generations. There is no other law that dictates our achievements and happiness in life as much as this law. This law is The Mirror Principle. Simply put the mirror principle states:

"Your Perception of Your Potential is Your Reality"

We could communicate this law as a scientific equation, which we will do a little later. We could illustrate this law in glowing philosophical terms, and perhaps we may do that. However, arguably the best way to understand and master this law is to use real life scenarios and show undeniable yet practical facts that support this law. The Mirror Principle is as real as the air you breathe; as unavoidable as death and taxes; as powerful as the sun.

The Mirror Principle: A Testament

Walter was a dreamer. He was born to a farmer who had failed several times at his business. Walter's father was a strict man. His insistence on education might have been somewhat overbearing but it made Walter and his siblings focus on their schoolwork. Soon, Walter took a keen interest in the arts. He found himself drawn to the art of sketching characters from the stories he had heard or made up. Although this was not a very popular talent at the time, he had a burning passion for drawing pictures that told a story.

At the tender age of eight, Walter would collect pennies from the neighbours who wanted him to draw pictures of their horses or other prized possessions. He soon met and made friends with a family of theatre lovers who introduced Walter to the world of motion pictures. Fascinated by that experience, Walter determined in his heart that all he wanted to spend his life doing was to create pictures that told a story. He sensed that there was power in storytelling, and wondered how beautiful it would be to tell interesting stories through active pictures.

Although the failing businesses of his father meant they had to move from Missouri to Kansas City and then to Chicago, he continued to get formal arts education in the local arts institutes. So while other kids busied themselves with the revelries of the day, Walter engaged in his passion. He studied at the Art Institute on Saturdays and many times at night. At high school he was the cartoonist of the school newspaper until he was forced to drop out of school at the age of 16. Yet all he had at the time was a dream; a dream of telling stories through pictures.

Soon hit by the reality of fending for himself, Walter resorted to driving an ambulance for the Red Cross. Restless from the lack of fulfilment from this job he packed up his bags and headed back to Kansas City to focus on his artistic career. He put together what he thought were fantastic picture stories, and applied for a job as a cartoonist with the local newspaper companies. One company after another rejected him preferring the more established cartoonists at the time. At some point, one newspaper editor scolded Walter saying, "Look, you lack any sense of imagination, and no good ideas can come from you". Not fazed, Walter carried on doing what he believed he knew how to do best. All he had was a dream of telling stories through pictures.

At the age of 19, Walter partnered with a friend to start up a business that provided commercial acts. Again the financial devil stared them in the face, and the business failed when they could not break even. Walter then picked up a job at a film company that made commercials based on animations. Fascinated by this field of storytelling Walter went into extensive research on how animated cartoons are made. At one point he had to beg his boss to allow him to study the animation cameras and perform experiments on them after work hours at home. Now armed with valuable information Walter set out to start yet another company. With just one employee, his Laugh O' Gram studios produced some low budget but unique cartoons. These cartoons were so good that they sold very quickly. He got the backing of a popular showman in Kansas City, and he allowed Walter to screen his cartoons in his local theatre. The cartoons became an instant hit.

Soon tragedy struck again; it was the old foe of financial distress that came calling. Laugh O'Gram studios could not cover the salaries of its growing employees and soon folded up. Walter took the hit and remained in Kansas City. In those dark days he busied himself with more drawings and taught himself ways of making his cartoons even better. All he had was a dream of telling stories through pictures.

Five years later, supported by his brother, Walter had managed to raise some funds to move to Hollywood, California to set up a studio. He sought sponsorship for some of his cartoon ideas, and after a few rejections his work was recognised by a New York distributor who gave him a distribution deal. This deal marked the turning point in Walter's career. Soon his productions were a popular delight across Hollywood and beyond. As more successful cartoons emerged from Walter's studio he invested funds into technology and designs. Soon his studio expanded and transformed into an empire. The uniqueness of his animations was the hallmark of this empire. The lessons learnt from past failures helped Walter to become a major force in world entertainment.

From being rejected by numerous experts to borrowing a camera from his work place so that he could learn at night, to facing the ridicule of failed ventures, Walter had now risen to the pinnacle of an industry that once mocked him. All he had was a dream of telling stories through pictures. His business empire would later spread into music production, publishing, merchandising, and television networks. Today his business stands as the largest media conglomerate in the world with tens of billions of US dollars in annual revenue. That man was Walt Disney.

Among the legendary works that were created by Walt Disney in those wilderness days at Kansas City are Mickey Mouse, Alice Comedies, Donald Duck, Popeye the Sailor, Snow White, Three Little Pigs, Oswald the Lucky Rabbit, and many more.

At the age of forty-five, Walt Disney would propose a project that formed an epitome of the dreams he had held onto from childhood. He suggested the incredible idea of Disneyland, and set out to build it. With the momentum of previous achievements behind him, Walter and his employees planned and built the Disneyland project in Florida. Walter would later reveal that his first visions of Disneyland came to him when as a teenager he had taken his sister to see the Electric Park some blocks away from their little home. Since then he saw an image of a huge theme park filled with fun activities for both the young and the old.

In exactly ten years, the project was completed. And so in one lifetime, one man's dream had become the reality of over five hundred million people who have been awed guests at the

The Mirror Principle

Disneyland Resort. When Disneyland Park opened in July of 1955, Walt Disney said to a joyous audience that included President Ronald Reagan:

> *"To all who came to this happy place; welcome. Disneyland is our land. Here age relives fond memories of the past.... And here youth may savour the challenges and promises of the future. Disneyland is dedicated to the ideals, the dreams and the hard facts that have created America....with hope that it would be a source of joy and inspiration to the entire world".*

This story is not yet another exposé on the rags-to-riches phenomenon. Rather, it is one of many outstanding examples of The Mirror Principle in operation. In fact The Mirror Principle works in all of our lives. The alarming thing is that it works whether we are aware of it or not. All our lives operate by The Mirror Principle. To those who understand and have mastered The Mirror Principle, it has brought them tremendous success. To those who have disregarded it, The Mirror Principle has brought them misery. The Mirror Principle is like all other natural laws. Take for instance the Law of Gravity. If you are unaware of gravity and you jumped off a cliff in an attempt to fly, the law will ensure that you come falling down to the ground. Your ignorance of the law does not mean it will fail to affect you. The law will take its course. People can use the law of gravity to their advantage when they respect it and understand how it works. On a positive note, just like all natural laws, The Mirror Principle can be understood and mastered.

> *"Your Perception of Your Potential is Your Reality"*
> *The Mirror Principle*

The Three Pillars of The Mirror Principle

The Mirror Principle is founded on three pillars. They are the Mirror, the Seed and the Mind.

In the story of Walt Disney we see The Mirror Principle in action. We do not even need other people's stories to illustrate The Mirror Principle. Our own lives are a product of The Mirror Principle and will always be. However, from other people's stories and achievements we can learn more about this timeless law.

The Mirror in Action

The mystique surrounding the mirror continues till this day. Its relevance in our everyday lives is huge. The mirror has had many meanings to many cultures from generation to generation. The mirror has played a big part in our lives; from how we view ourselves to seeing things that the normal eyes are unable to see. In a sense the mirror is our judge. In another sense, it is our third eye. Through the mirror we see an image of ourselves that gets imprinted on our hearts and minds. It also shows us details and angles that our physical eyesight is limited in reaching.

There is such a power in the mirror that it has the innate ability to make you become what it shows to you. The mirror is a catalyst for transformation; so much so that Scryers believed it had healing powers and diviners allege that it traps the souls of the dead. When you look into a mirror it tells you who you are. The image you possess of yourself is essentially the picture that your mirror provided to you. We have come to trust the mirror to tell us who we are. Our mental image of ourselves is the reflection we saw in the mirror.

When the mirror tells us that we are scruffy, or that we do not look up to scratch we believe it like a patient believes a doctor. We see the little details which the mirror shows us and we make corrections. We live our lives and relate with people based on the image that the mirror has presented to us. The mirror shows us our weaknesses that we could change, and strengths that give us confidence. We owe most of our worries and happiness to the mirror. And there is absolutely nothing wrong with that. After all, the mirror never lies; it is our truest friend.

The Mirror Principle does not derive its use of the mirror in a physical sense. The concept of the mirror is beyond the concept of a silver-coated looking glass hanging on your bedroom wall. The glass mirror on your wall tells you about your physical looks. Like a loyal servant, it speaks back to you as you change your hairstyle or adjust the knot on your tie. However the concept of the mirror transcends these physical checks. As there is a mirror for the body, there is also a mirror for the soul. You may call it The Mind's Mirror. Not everyone has a mirror in his or her bedrooms but everyone is born with a mirror in their minds. It is this mirror that we look into more than any other mirror that exists. The mind's mirror is not made of glass and silver coating; it is made up of our imagination and beliefs.

The Mind's Mirror: The fate of us all

Much more than the physical mirror, the mind's mirror tells us who we are, and reminds us of it every passing hour of our lives. The mind's mirror is so powerful that all our actions, our dreams and our inspiration in life are dependent on it. Our lives are a result of the pictures we see in this mirror. As it has always been with mirrors, they control us. Our mental mirrors hold our impression about ourselves. They determine our self-image. The better the image you see on that mirror the happier you feel as a person. Even more significantly the mirror has the innate ability to transform you into what it says you are.

The logical explanation behind the mirror's powers is remarkably simple. You look in the mirror and it tells you who you are. You believe it because it is a mirror; it never lies. Once you accept its verdict on you, all you do revolves around that image of you. Let us take a practical example. I once lived in a block of apartments. It was one of those blocks of flats where the builders thought it was a mark of genius to fit mirrors into the elevators. For some reason the mirrors in the lifts made everyone look like their bodies had been badly inflated with a pump. You got into the lifts, and the reflection of a monster was staring right back at you. It was hilarious; troubling to some. I know the feeling of near depression I felt anytime I got into those elevators, and stared at my reflection. I then imagined how depressing it would have been if I had no previous knowledge about how I looked. The mental image I would have had about myself would have been distorted and depressing. I perhaps would have had a lower expectation out of life, and in this world where there is so much emphasis on grooming and physical appearance, my mind would have told me I had little chance.

That is a simple example of how mirrors control our lives. They dictate our moods and our sense of self. To a large extent mirrors shape our self-image and our altitudes in life.

Shaping The Tool That Shapes Us

Did you know that these days, there are mirrors that are specially designed to make you feel better about yourself? We tend to forget that perception is reality. Who says that you are a monster? Nobody but your mind. I am sure I have walked into some high street shops, and I have come out of them feeling like Prince Charming. All that happened in that shop was a mirror; built and fitted in such a way that when I saw myself, it emphasised the grace of my appearance and nothing else. I immediately felt great about myself and life suddenly felt, smelt and tasted better. Well, until I got back to my apartment block and into those lifts. But you get the point. It may not be the only thing that dictates our confidence but the physical mirror has quite an influence.

Now, by far more powerful than the physical mirror is the mind's mirror. It is there all the time. We cannot avoid it. Many people have a solid resolve around their physical appearance so they are not moved by the reflections on the physical mirror. Whether or not you are affected by the physical mirror, you are certainly under the influence of your mind's mirror. Every living person has a mind's mirror. It is the mental image of who you think you are now and whom you think you could become in the future. The mind's mirror is the mirror created by our beliefs and imagination. Just like the physical mirror drives people's impression about their physical looks the mind's mirror drives all your views about your personality and your entire life. After all the fuss made about mirrors, it is amazing to realise that the most powerful mirror lies in our minds.

Have you ever thought for one moment that you can create your own mirror and make it show you what you want to see? Put in more concise terms, have you ever realised that you can create the very thing that controls your life? Think about it.

The physical mirror on your bedroom wall may control the way you feel about your body but the mind's mirror controls your entire life. The amazing truth is that the mind's mirror is an object of your own creation. Whether you are unaware of it or you are vaguely interested in it, the mind's mirror is consistently being created by you. It is this same mirror that you would look into every hour of every day of your life to assess your own reflection. What the mind's mirror says of you is what you always become. It is your fate. The mirror never lies; it never fails.

A well-dressed woman suffering from the heartache of rejection could look into the physical mirror. Although it tells her "you look lovely and irresistible", the image of a rejected woman is passing her a different message from her mind's mirror. There is no amount of preaching that the physical mirror can do; she will not feel confident about herself because the minds mirror is always more powerful. On the flip side, a scruffy looking fellow who knows in his mind that he is loved and admired acts with full confidence. He will have happiness as the mind's mirror always wins. This is why the world has its suicidal rich and happy poor. The mind's mirror is the captain of the ship aboard which our lives set sail.

In the eyes of The Mirror Principle the mirror is a vision statement; a reflection of what one is about and what one could become. Whether it is a picture etched on a canvas or words scribbled on a yellow-sticky, or an idea indelibly printed on your mind, your mirror is a vision statement. It tells you who you are on the inside and shows you what you shall soon become. Again, this mirror can consist of anything. It may be the hopeless image of forever living in addiction and depravity. It could be an image of despair, rejection and lack of skill. It may be a happy picture of achievement and ability; or a picture of giving and fulfilment. Have no doubt about it; the image is who you are and what you shall become. The mirror never lies; it never fails.

Sages Elixir

"The human mind is a channel through which things-to-be are coming into the realms of things that are"

Henry Ford

In the story of Walt Disney, his mirror is quite evident. It was captured in those words, "I will tell great stories through pictures". Etched at the back of his mind, the mind's mirror was created by these words. It propelled him from rejection by local editors in Kansas City to becoming the leader of the world's highest earning media institution. Disney may not have had a physical mirror on his bedroom wall, but he understood the mirror that mattered the most; the mirror in the mind; a mirror so easily created and yet so powerful.

The mirror is a vision; a created dream; a portrait of your beliefs and imagination; a third eye. It looks beyond the present and shows you not just who you are but who you shall be in the years to come.

Sages Elixir

"Hold a picture of yourself long and steadily enough in your mind's eye and you would be drawn to it"

Napoleon Hill

The Seed in Action

Everyone is born with an interest. Even where that interest is hard to figure out, everyone is born with ability. Your abilities and lines of interest will ultimately guide you to what you may do to live a worthwhile life.

In the eyes of The Mirror Principle, the seed is your ability or passion. The seed is the closest allegory to human purpose. As you study the seed you are bound to see striking similarities between a seed and the human purpose. The balance of the universe is so amazing that it has solicited many theories and arguments. As different plants support each other for survival in the universe so do human beings have seeds of purpose that support each other. This way the balance of the universe is maintained.

Every human being is unique, and this says something about how we are all part of one complete picture. No matter when, how or where you were born, you have a seed in you that the world needs. It may sound too good to be true but it is true. The universe is incomplete without you. There are people in the world whose lives are meant to benefit from the seed you have within you.

Some may argue that they have no skills. They look at the millions of skillsets that inundate human existence, and they say, "I am a jack of all trades and master of none" or "I am not particularly good at anything". The universe's reply to them is "Well then, create one that you are good at". Skillsets are infinite. You are either good at one that already exists, or you create one that comes natural to you. Remember that the celebrated skills of today all began with certain persons who rolled up their sleeves and said, "This might work". The things we celebrate today; the arts, poetry, governance policies, music, smart gadgets, dance types, games, medicine, novels, the movie industry, automobiles and many more all started off with people who followed after their passion.

Sages Elixir

"People see things that are and ask why; but I see things that are not and ask why not"

Robert F. Kennedy

Even when you think you have no skill you may look to your passions as a clue to your seed of purpose. Sometimes your seed is buried amongst your lines of interest. What you like is an indication of what you were born to do. Little wonder why you feel happiest when you are engaging in something you love to do.

In the story told of Walt Disney, his seed was "drawing pictures to tell stories". Not everyone likes to draw. I for one do not enjoy drawing. It does not come naturally to me. I admire good paintings or sketches, but I would probably run mad if I was made to paint for my dear life. In the case of young Walter drawing fascinated him. He felt a rush of blood anytime he had a chance to draw. To me, and a billion others, this would have been a chore. To Walter, he relished the idea of painting, and did this with relative ease. Your seed is in you. All you have to do is recognise it and then do it. Whether you are a young Walter or a much older Grandma Moses, the seed is in you.

Some argue that their seed is insufficient; not significant enough to make them survive the financial obligations of today's world. They say things like "All I like to do is make cupcakes. And that is not going to put food on the table or pay the rent. So I do my real job and then I do my hobby on the side. It is the boring job that brings in the money. My hobby is just a pastime I enjoy."

This is where we misconstrue the idea of money. Never forget that money is a creation of man simply because of the need to trade. In other words, money is paper that stamps a value on everything. So when you have something that someone else wants, if they want it badly enough, they will give that paper called money so that they can have what they want. If you agree to this then always remember this next line because it might change your concept of money forever.

"Money is only a paper symbol of wealth and wealth is inside of you."

If people like what is inside of you enough they shall be willing to pay money to make use of that wealth. Your seed is your wealth. Depending on how much you nurture your seed, its wealth is obvious to the world. It is the nature of the world to place a value on things. Your wealth's value depends on how much effort you have put into your seed.

Nobody paid a dime to Bill Gates when he was a school dropout; an ambitious programmer at the age of 16. Today he has taken his passion for computers to such a height that people pay him as much as three thousand US Dollars per minute to tap into his wealth. Nobody paid a thousand dollars for the paintings of young Damien Hirst when he first started out, but twenty years on, his artworks are auctioned at tens of millions of British Pounds. Not many spared their money to watch a 15 year old Michael Jordan when all he had was a seed of sporting talent. He pressed on with that seed of purpose. Within a few years many people were splashing out millions of US Dollars to be entertained by the finished product. The list goes on and on.

The Mirror Principle cannot tell you what your seed is. However, it assures you that you have a seed; it shows you how you can use your seed to live the fulfilled life that you desire. Your seed does not need to bring you millions of dollars like Gates, Jordan or Hirst but one eternal guarantee is that your seed will look after you. Fulfilment does not come solely from money, but unleashing your seed gives you a sense of happiness that nothing in the world can replace. In other words your seed gives you value. All it demands is for you to recognise it; nurture it and it will come back to nurture you.

Imagine yourself to be a farmer. You have a seed whose life is at the mercy of your decision. You take that seed and you plant it. You cultivate it and watch it grow. You give it water and sunlight. You remove the weeds from around it that might attack it as it grows into a full mature plant. When the tree matures you will have for yourself, a big strong tree, or perhaps an entire forest as you keep cultivating. At this point the tree begins to take care of itself and its fruits sustain you. You suddenly realise that you do not need to put in so much effort anymore. The tree has begun to work for you. It could give you food, fulfilment or even shelter. Such is the seed of purpose. Once you cultivate it, it grows and in a short while it starts to take care of you.

You would probably agree that the toughest time for any beautiful plant is when it is only a seed. In that young state it is just a seed. There is nothing fancy about it. A seed's beauty lies not in its present state but in what it could become. This is why seeds are easily ignored and sometimes lost. They do not look like much but within them lays a beautiful garden. Seeds of purpose are most at risk when they lie in us; untapped and constrained from showing what they truly are.

We do need to understand that there is a big difference between fulfilment and achievement. An achievement is a successful effort that may or may not bring you personal happiness; a fulfilment is an effort that brings you satisfaction and happiness. We shall touch on this difference with more practical examples later on. If you ever accomplish something that does not bring you fulfilment it is an indication that you have not used your seed of purpose. This is possible because we are so blessed with ability that we can actually do things outside of our passions and interests. For instance, I have taken up jobs in the past not because I was totally interested in them but because I felt obliged to do them. And I did those jobs rather well; or at least I think I did. These accomplishments did not make me happy or fill me with satisfaction even though I completed them. They were not connected to my seed of purpose. Even in being successful at these things fulfilment was elusive.

This is the subtle difference between living a life of fulfilment and living a life of unhappy conformity. The multiplicity of abilities in us humans was meant to be a gift; a gift which has become a curse that makes men to settle for less. This is a clear and present danger; an enemy to true purpose. Our seed of purpose is the only key to our fulfilment. Your seed is your ability. It is your passion. It is who you were born to be. It is the reason you are here. Recognise it; nurture it; keep it safe from the weeds of life. Let it grow and your fulfilment will no longer be a distant dream.

The Mind In Action

The most powerful energy in the world is not the fuel that propels a rocket into the skies. The most potent energy under man's immediate control is mental energy. There are over 7 billion people in the world. Each person produces millions of thoughts every day. Our world is inundated by these thought signals. Like every energy particle our thoughts obey the laws of attraction and resonance. We inadvertently draw to ourselves experiences and events that are connected to our most dominant thoughts.

Imagine all that has ever been built or achieved; they were a result of thought energy. Your decision making process is your mind at work. Your emotions, calculations and imaginations are all depictions of your mind at work. Nothing happens by accident. The mind creates it. The car you are driving today, the stylish clothes you are wearing and the breath you are taking all started from a single thought.

There is no telling where thoughts can go when we release them. They are so potent that once well structured, they form a force that conquers the world. I remember testing the power of the sun's rays using a glass. Just merely holding up the glass over a piece of paper, the paper gathered so much heat that it was aflame in minutes. I had learnt one of life's stunning lessons; the power of focus. The glass had diverted the sun's rays into one single line of heat energy; so fierce that it burnt up the paper. The same way, everything ever built or achieved is a result of intense mental energy. Such is the nature of the mind in action.

We know that the best things in life are free, but come with responsibility. The mind in all its beauty and power is a gift to us all. It also demands some measure of responsibility. This stems from the fact that the mind is a massive battleground. The mind is surrounded by so much information, and it lives on information. So at every point in time there is a battle amongst all kinds of thoughts trying to grab the limelight in our mind. Such is the nature of energy. Energy is constantly fighting for a place. The mind is flooded by so much thought that it is always processing thought energy whether you are consciously thinking or unconscious. So even when you are asleep your mind is constantly releasing and receiving mental energy. The thought that generates the strongest emotion in your mind is what many experts now refer to as your dominant thought.

The Mirror Principle

Like the glass in the sun, if you can steady the mind to focus under the influence of certain thoughts, the results are often monumental. In other words thought is supreme. Your dominant thought controls your reality. In the eyes of The Mirror Principle, the mind plays a key role in bringing you to your aim. The mind is a facilitator; a springboard that carries you to a desired height. Like the springboard, the more you press upon it the higher you tend to reach.

We have learnt that it is not the thoughts we are aware of that affect us the most; it is the thoughts we are not thinking; the mental energy released and received by our subconscious mind. This is what attracts most of our experiences into our lives. How do these subtle thoughts get built? They are a heap of every dominant thought we have had for every single moment since birth. Like a sponge dipped into water would soak water and then release water even under the least pressure, so does our mind retain the thoughts that we let in, and release these thoughts even when we are not aware.

Sages Elixir

"What lies behind us and what lies before us are tiny matters compared to what lies within us"

Ralph W. Emerson

In the story told of Walt Disney, we can vividly see the mind in action. Walt Disney busied his mind with his dream and thoughts of how to achieve this dream. He never veered off from that path of thought. He may or may not have understood the importance of mind and thought but he sure demonstrated it. What makes us sure of this? History and science show that only a sustained pattern of thought can result in any significant achievement. Walter kept his dream alive in his mind. He dwelt on these lofty thoughts, and soon the thoughts drove him. In spite of discouraging situations, negative reviews and hostile events he was not a man to be deterred. His mind was focused on his goal. Walt Disney is only one of a pristine group of people who have harnessed the power of the human mind to fulfil their potential.

So was Walter's mind always on the prize; never faltering? No. This is humanly impossible. Did he have conflicting thoughts or consider quitting? Of course he did. So how did he succeed? The answer is simple. His dominant thought was of his dream. Your reality does not fluctuate with every thought. Your reality only conforms to your dominant thought; the persistent thoughts in your subconscious. In a sense it is not the thoughts you are thinking this minute that counts; it is the environment of your mind. You could have momentary negative thoughts as all humans do, but it is the prevailing attitude of your mind; that predominant mental energy which propels you to success. Walter had his fair share of disappointments and doubts, but he let his dream become his dominant thought.

Our dominant thoughts do turn around to work for us. It is very much like creating a powerful robotic servant that turns around to serve you. There is enough proof in this book to show that our dominant thoughts attract people and events into our lives. Was it a coincidence that Walter had neighbours who were such art lovers that they were willing to pay him to draw for them? I think not. Surely, it could not have been a coincidence that potential studio owners crossed paths with Walter early on during his journey to fulfilment.

Habits are formed as a direct result of dominant thoughts; thoughts impressed into our subconscious through consistent practice. The mind records the intensity and patterns of each thought. Without warning, it reproduces these thoughts into our lives like a programmed fireworks display. Your habits either make or break you. Habits have no regard for your conscious intentions. They just respond to the events that stimulate them. Through deep or repeated conscious thoughts, dominant thoughts take control over your life.

Two men inherit a thousand dollars. One instantly hits the streets to purchase a month's supply of heroine. This would keep him in high spirits for the next few weeks even though it is wrecking his life. The second man instantly thinks of getting a better golf set that could take his golf career to a new level. A few years afterwards, one man is on a sick bed and fighting his misery; the other is lifting a trophy as the winner of a local golf tournament. Here we see two men with the same resources but different habits; two different outcomes.

Your thought patterns determine your altitude in life. When you continue to think a particular thought long enough, it gathers tremendous mental energy. Soon, unknown to you it starts to attract things on your behalf. It starts to control your life. Like the autopilot it drives you; even when you are not conscious of where you are going it is taking you there anyway. So treat your mind with respect; apply it with caution and use it to your advantage. It is your greatest asset. Teach it fear and soon fear shall take root in your life; fill it with joy and soon joy becomes the predominant force in your life.

The Mirror Principle: It Even Has Its Own Mathematical Equation

Laws are remarkable. Laws respect nobody and they show no favours. For as long as certain conditions are met the law must run its course. The Mirror Principle is a law of life; as real as the laws of thermodynamics or motion. It has three simple conditions. Once these three conditions are satisfied the accomplishment of your mission is guaranteed. First let us restate The Mirror Principle.

> *"Your Perception of Your Potential is Your Reality"*
> *The Mirror Principle*

Think about it. Let us get our geeky hats out, and state The Mirror Principle in a mathematical equation. It will read thus:

```
Perception x Potential = Reality;
```

Or we could rewrite the equation as:

```
Reality = Potential Perception;
```

The equation is somewhat unusual but true; simple but very powerful. The Mirror Principle states that your potential by itself is nothing. On the other hand, your reality is inevitable. By this I mean that everyone must have a reality as long as they are alive. However, reality is not constant. The Mirror Principle states that the determining factor of reality is perception. The reality of any person is a product of their perception and potential.

Let us briefly define these three components of our lives. In the Webster's Dictionary:

1. Potential is defined as "the inherent capacity for coming into being";
2. Perception is defined as "the quality, state, or capability, of being affected by something external";
3. Reality is defined as "that which is real; an actual existence; that which is not imagination, fiction, or pretence; that which has objective existence, and is not merely an idea".

There is a useful allegory for the three pillars of The Mirror Principle. They are not new to us. They are: The Mirror, The Seed and The Mind.

The Mirror points to Reality;
The Seed aptly depicts Potential and
The Mind refers to Perception.

These are the three pillars upon which The Mirror Principle stands. The Mirror, the Seed and the Mind; these three pillars come together in the most subliminal way to symbolize the fate of all human endeavours.

The life of every person, organisation or nation rests on a tripod. This tripod refers to the three pillars of The Mirror Principle. The purpose of this book is to make you aware of this tripod, and to use The Mirror Principle to your advantage. The truth is whether you use it or not, The Mirror Principle is already in operation in your life. Why not then use it to your advantage? Why not use it for your benefit? Why not use it to become a blessing to your world? Why not use it to achieve success and happiness?

So does this mean that happiness can be guaranteed? The answer is yes; if we use The Mirror Principle the right way. It takes practice and trust but even where men have failed laws never fail. They are always there; guaranteed to deliver a certain result as long as certain conditions are passed. Let us take a look at the three conditions upon which The Mirror Principle is founded.

The Conditions of The Mirror Principle

1. Locate your seed;
2. Have a mirror;
3. Use your mind.

The first condition is to "locate your seed". This is the starting point in taking advantage of The Mirror Principle. The seed is the first of three legs upon which any fulfilling achievement stands. The Mirror Principle requires the seed of your potential to begin its work. Just as an orange seed is the raw material needed to produce an orange tree so is your potential the raw material needed to produce your fulfilling achievement. As has been demonstrated earlier, you can achieve many things and remain unhappy; bound by a feeling of discontent. This happens when you have not followed your seed of purpose. You have potential to do many things, but only the potential that is tied to your true purpose would bring you to the contentment that you seek. The Mirror Principle can be applied to any kind of potential you have. On these pages, the focus is on how The Mirror Principle could be applied to your seed of purpose. This book is not only interested in showing you a roadmap to achievement, but also in sharing with you a tested recipe for personal fulfilment.

Every person has a seed of purpose; something that gets you excited; something that can keep you awake at night. Maybe it is something you do with relative ease; something you do easily even where others struggle. This is your seed of promise. Many times, as the possessor of this seed, it is easy to suppress your seed with doubt. This is a normal temptation but you must resist it. Many seed owners do not believe in the power of their own seed. They take to the negatives rather than embrace the positives. They think it is a good virtue to rubbish the skills or passions that make them unique; a sort of misplaced modesty. Think about it. If you have a seed then it was meant to bless people. If you hide it or disregard it, you are not only depriving yourself of satisfaction but you are depriving others; people whose lives to some degree would have benefitted from your purpose. Developing what you are good at is not a sign of arrogance or selfishness. On the contrary, it is an act of courage and selflessness.

So how do you locate your seed of purpose? The indicators are everywhere around you. Some of us already know our purpose. We may not be doing it right now but we know our seed of purpose just like we know our names. For those who claim not to know, ask yourself the following twelve questions. As you sincerely answer these questions you would begin to find a common thread that runs through these answers; a common theme at the back of your mind; your seed of purpose.

1. What have you done in the past that brought you tremendous joy?
2. What do others compliment you for anytime you do it?

3. What did you love to do when you were only a child?
4. If you had all the money in the world and the best of everything, what would you still be doing just because you love it?
5. What do you feel comfortable doing that others envy you for?
6. What do you do easily that others find difficult - In other words what are your skills?
7. Who are your role models – whose accomplishments would you like to remake in your own life?
8. What do people come to you for – Perhaps something they feel you know or do better?
9. If you were told to speak about anything; anything at all and guaranteed that everyone would listen to you with keen interest; what would it be?
10. What do you value the most in your life?
11. Picture you were 85 years old, and extremely happy with no regrets of things left undone; how must you have lived your life?
12. What causes do you easily connect with or believe in?

Some seeds of purpose could be specific. Others could be quite vague. No matter the seed, The Mirror Principle will bring that seed to fulfilment. One person's seed of purpose might be as specific as owning a successful grocery shop in a local area, while another may be as a vague as being a part of anything that improves people's lives. The Mirror Principle will work for both. One may desire to be a respected chef known all over the world, while another may dream of spending their lives as a volunteer worker in a village in Africa. The Mirror Principle will take both of them there. Again, your seed does not have to be bound to your local community or place of birth. The world is a huge stage; there are over seven billion people in the world. Your purpose is relevant to some of these people. They might be halfway around the world from you, but you will never know until you locate your seed.

Use the answers to the twelve questions to locate your seed. If doing something makes you smile; then hold on to it. The amazing thing is that The Mirror Principle will take you to its fulfilment, and you could live a life filled with smiles.

Sages Elixir

"Your task is to discover your work, and then with all your heart to give yourself to it"

Buddha

The second condition is to "have a mirror". We mentioned earlier that all of us have a mirror inside our minds. It is the mind's mirror. The Mirror Principle is constantly at work in our lives. It makes use of the image we maintain in the mind's mirror. However, to have a fulfilled life you need to ensure that your mind's mirror is the right one. The mirror is your mental image of yourself. It controls how you respond to everything and as such it is the biggest contributor to the heights you can reach in life.

If you have a mirror of hopelessness and poverty it is certain that you would live in hopelessness and uncertainty. The Mirror Principle is so powerful that even if somebody else changes your reality you will shortly be back to the reflection in your mind's mirror. So let us assume that you see a reflection of a poor and hopeless man in your mind's mirror. Even if someone nice comes into your life and changes your physical state by giving you a load of riches, The Mirror Principle guarantees that as long as you maintain that mirror in your mind you will be back to poverty and hopelessness in a short time. So in effect, The Mirror Principle says, "What you see is what you get".

When the phrase, "have a mirror", is used as a condition for The Mirror Principle it is actually making you aware of the effect your mirror has on the results in your life. So it is not merely saying for you to have a mirror because you already have one. It is saying for you to have the right mirror.

The Mirror Principle

You should have the right image of yourself. The starting point of your fulfilment might be the seed but the mirror is equally important. It is the mirror that places a demand on the seed. The mirror shows your seed everything that your seed can become. If the seed is an unborn child in the womb then the mirror is the full-grown man; the finished article. The mirror shows you all you can become. It tells you where you are going; it shows you as much detail as you are willing to see. The mirror has the answers to all the questions you may have on your journey to true success. The mirror is your future state. It is a reflection of who you truly are. It never shows you the raw seed that you are now; rather your mirror shows you the finished work that you should become.

The amazing thing about the mind's mirror is that it is completely a creation of your own mind. We have the gift to create our mirror, and paint it with the colours that we wish.

Sages Elixir

"Imagination is more important than knowledge. Knowledge is limited. Imagination encircles the world."
Albert Einstein

For The Mirror Principle to work in our favour and bring us tremendous success, we must dream of all that our seed can achieve. We have one of the mind's most potent tools at our disposal, and that is our imagination. Imagination is a creative form of mental energy. It creates pictures. It is our connection between our present lives and the things that we could bring into our lives.

Your most dominant dream of whom you were born to be and the things you can do soon become the mirror you have firmly etched in your mind. The mythical representation of mirrors throughout the history of mankind is not all hogwash. The mirror possesses magical powers to the extent that it changes you to become what it shows you.

Your mirror is your vision statement. It is what you could become. The Mirror Principle says that as long as that mirror remains the same you will become what the mirror says. Your mirror is your goal; your target; where you aim to be in the near future.

Your mirror does not have to be stored at the back of your mind alone. The mirror can be reproduced on a piece of paper or on a wall. Your mirror can be stored anywhere as long as you can see it. Your mirror should be in front of you all the time. Although the mirror is in your mind, it is constantly under attack from other images that seek to gain dominance over your chosen mirror. This is why reproducing your chosen mirror on papers, walls, and anything your senses can reach is

The Mirror Principle

vitally important. These things are an extension of the mind's mirror; they reinforce what you hold true about yourself. Remember that "Whatever the eye sees and the ear hears the mind believes". It does not matter if your mirror is written in words or sketched in pictures. It does not matter how great the image on the mirror is. The Mirror Principle guarantees that as far as the three conditions are met, those words or pictures will soon become your reality.

Sages Elixir

"Your imagination is your preview of life's coming attractions"

Albert Einstein

"Through imagination we can visualize the uncreated worlds of potential that lie within us"

Stephen Covey

There is the third and final condition that says, "use your mind". The mind is the third leg of the tripod upon which any significant accomplishment stands. Your mind is your mental energy. We have studied some astonishing facts about the mind, and how it is at the centre of the experiences we encounter and the things we do.

The mind is like a battlefield. There is an ever-present war between your seed of purpose and other pressures in your life going on in your mind. The Mirror Principle requires you to focus your mental energy on your goal. As you concentrate your mind on the reflection in the mirror, The Mirror Principle ensures that you become the image in the mirror. The Mirror Principle works immensely with mental energy. It assures that your dominant perception becomes your reality. If your dominant perception is built around your seed of purpose then your purpose becomes your reality. If your dominant perception is filled with hate and disillusion then anger becomes your inevitable reality.

The Three Pillars of Our Lives

Our lives are always standing on these three pillars: The Seed which holds our potential, The Mirror which is a picture of who we think we are or can be, and The Mind which contains our perception or beliefs. The mirror eventually becomes our reality. Interestingly, The Mirror Principle does not discriminate between good or bad; weak or strong. If you have potential, whether you use that potential to aid or harm people, The Mirror Principle will work for you. If you use your potential weakly, The Mirror Principle is present to give you weak results. If you use the whole of your potential, The Mirror Principle is also on hand to give you a wholesome result. So the great news is that if we find that thing which brings us great joy, no matter the adverse conditions, if we put our mind to it and maintain a picture of us achieving that goal, The Mirror Principle will bring it to pass.

If the mirror is a destination and the seed is a starting point then your mind is the vehicle that takes you there. If you have a lifelong dream but at the moment all you have is your dream, then you have found a good starting point. Beautify that dream as much as your imagination would allow you. Hold that dream in front of you and never lose sight of it. Focus your mind and its extraordinary energy on thoughts around your dream. Let the dream drive you. Once you have a dream and you devote your energy to that dream, The Mirror Principle gives you a certain assurance that one day that dream will not only be alive in your mind but evident in the form of an achievement for everyone to see.

If all you are is a mere seed of promise but what you seek is a garden of achievement then your mind is the soil on which the growth must take place. By using the powerful reservoir of mental energy stored within us we can provide the fertile ground that transforms a seed into a beautiful garden. There is no other facilitator as great as the human mind. You are only as great as your mirror; only as accomplished as your thoughts; only truly happy doing something connected to your seed.

Having a formidable mirror is as vital to a great mind as a nice soundtrack is to a good movie. Your mirror is the melody that your life will sing along to; the rhythm you will dance to. It is important for the right melody to flood your mind. Once your mind picks a dominant rhythm, The Mirror Principle sets to work like a loyal servant. The Mirror Principle assures that if you focus long enough on the image of your dreams held in your mind's mirror, there is only one outcome: You will be propelled from your present state into a new fulfilling reality.

Many people use the term 'breakthrough' a lot in reference to achieving something they have always desired. It is also helpful to see breakthrough as leaping from your present circumstances, and breaking through the looking glass of your finished image. The mirror is your destination, and you have the power in your mind to break into the mirror of who you can become.

Responsibility is another word we are all too familiar with. Whether we first heard it from our parents or teachers or on the news in reference to our leaders, the word responsibility is inevitable. The Mirror Principle brings a fresh definition to the term. Responsibility could be broken down into two words: Response and Ability. Response is what you do and ability is what you can do. So your responsibility is actually your 'response ability'. Furthermore your ability refers to your seed of purpose. Your response is determined by how highly you rate your ability. Your response ability is essentially the image you hold in your mind. In a sense, your mirror is your responsibility.

Your goal or vision statement is your responsibility. If you can see it and you can believe that you will achieve it then you are certain to achieve it. You have got the response ability in you for everything your imagination can create around your seed of purpose. Your responsibility places a demand on your seed of potential, and your mind helps you to get there.

Sages Elixir

"We succeed only as we identify in life, or in war, or in anything else a single overriding objective, and we make all considerations bend to that objective"

Gen Dwight Eisenhower

"I have learned that if one advances confidently in the direction of his dreams and endeavours to live the life he

has imagined, he would meet with a success unexpected in common hours"

Henry Thoreau

"The future belongs to those who believe in the beauty of their dreams"

Eleanor Roosevelt

Nutshell

Picture a seed, and a bare garden, and a mirror. The seed already exists within us. The bare garden is your mind. The mirror is a reflection of the beautiful garden that the seed can produce. These three things are within us. They are the three pillars of The Mirror Principle; the powerful tripod stand of our lives.

Our reality or circumstances in life are a product of these three forces coming together. First your mind exists as a bare garden. It is waiting to blossom. It is bustling with unbelievable amounts of mental energy. The mind is potent; it is the seat of your emotions, memory and beliefs. It dictates your actions. It relies on the thought that is most dominant within it to interact with the world around you. This dominant thought is a form of mental energy. Even while you sleep it drives the mind to communicate with other forms of energy within the universe. In this sphere, like attracts like. Your dominant thought attracts your reality. In essence the mind creates your reality.

Secondly there is the seed; your purpose in the universe. Make no mistake about it; the universe is one of the most organized conundrums you could ever imagine. Our universe does not exist in chaos. Every person, indeed every living thing carries a seed of purpose that maintains a balance in the universe. Your seed is unique to you, and it has a purpose. There are many things that point to your seed. Your childhood passions, your natural skillsets, and your lines of interest all point to what you were born to do.

Lastly but not least is the mirror. It is your self-image; your perception of who you are and what you can become. Your seed is constant; the determining factor of how great your seed becomes is your mirror; your perception of it. This perception is your self-image; the mental mirror. As you perceive your seed so shall your mind act, and so shall your reality be formed.

The most valuable gift that we have been born with is not really the mirror. It is the gift of being able to create the reflection in the mirror. In a sense, we have been blessed with the power to be all we want to be. Even for those who ignore

The Mirror Principle they are still obeying it. The Mirror Principle is a part and parcel of our lives; it is what makes us who we are.

5 The Mirror Principle In Action

In life there are achievements and there are worthwhile achievements. If a man born with a passion for building houses is forced by circumstances to work as a lawyer, he would likely attain a number of noble achievements, and earn enough money to live comfortably; but he will never be fulfilled. He may become a successful lawyer, but he will be far from fulfilled. So as humans we have the potential to do many things but we have only one purpose. The Mirror Principle works with potential. So even when we are working outside of our purpose, as long as you have the potential to perform a certain task and believe that you can, The Mirror Principle works to bring it to reality; it knows no better. To have a worthwhile achievement that makes you feel fulfilled, it is your duty to find your purpose, and put your potentials to work around that purpose. Almost as certain as night and day, The Mirror Principle ensures that your belief in your purpose will be your reality; it pays no attention to how noble or how great that belief is.

There are hardly any significant achievements in the history of mankind that do not have the imprints of The Mirror Principle. Show me a human achievement, and I will show you the presence of The Mirror Principle. The Mirror Principle is as timeless as it is effective. However, this is not a book that seeks to celebrate big feats only. Wisdom dictates that those who accomplish meaningful but uncelebrated feats are as great as those whose feats dazzle the entire world. That said, we sometimes illustrate the effects of a great law using the lives of famous people simply because their stories are well documented; not because they are greater than any other person who found their purpose and fulfilled it.

The notable figures or the celebrated men and women across generations all used a common principle to accomplish their feats; feats for which they are either praised or condemned. Whether they are regarded as heroes or villains they are history's sculptors; remembered for achieving feats that have shaped human existence till this day.

***

Alexander Graham Bell was born into a family of elocutionists in Scotland in 1847. His father like all educated parents at the time enrolled young Alex into conventional school. Little Alex dropped out only after completing his fourth year at the school. He was less than average on his grades, and was often reported as absent from class much to the chagrin of his father. The reason for his poor performance was not farfetched. Alex had a stronger passion for science than the structured syllabus of the school could give to him. He was particularly fascinated with the world of acoustics; the science of sounds.

As his beloved mother developed partial deafness, Alex's interest in the field of sound waves and vibrations deepened. He sensed that he could become an inventor and went about his passion from a young age. Although his elder brother was already achieving good success in the family tradition of elocution, all that young Alex could see himself becoming was an inventor; a man that sees needs and builds machines to meet those needs.

At age 12, Alex had visited a neighbour's flour mill and questioned why the act of dehusking of the wheat took so many man-hours and so much strenuous effort. Within days, using only rotating paddles and a set of nail brushes, he constructed a dehusking machine that operated on that farm for many years.

At 16, Alex secured a position as a music and elocution teacher at the Weston House Academy. In his spare hours he devoted his mind to experiments around sound and electricity. He attended science exhibitions, read tons of books about the mechanics of sounds and even sent compilations of his findings to the subject matter experts of his day. From some of these experts he courted ridicule but from others who recognised the uniqueness of his work, they gave him advice and encouragement.

Just as Alex was about to establish himself as a scientist, tragedy struck his family. Tuberculosis struck his entire household and Alex was poor in health. Death took a hold of his two surviving brothers. The Bells had to seek treatment halfway around the world in Canada. They arrived in Canada almost empty handed. Yet Alex had three things that no circumstance could take away from him: his potential, his dream and his determination. Despite his frail conditions, Alex aged 23, set out to continue his scientific work using very limited laboratory equipment. It is a fact that back then in a large hollow place nestled among trees at Tutela Heights, Ontario, Canada, Alex set up his workshop, which he called "The Dreaming Place".

After four years of disappointments and hard work, Alex devised and patented the ground-breaking acoustic telegraph that would later symbolize the birth of the telephone. In 1876, Alex publicly demonstrated his astonishing invention to an awed audience that included Emperor Pedro II of Brazil and many notable scientists. Soon his invention caught the interest of Queen Victoria who invited him to a private audience. She was said to have described Alex's work as "most extraordinary". In 1877, the Bell Telephone Company was formed. By the end of the 19th century over a million telephone lines were in use across America. The rest as they say is now history.

> *"Your Perception of Your Potential is Your Reality"*
> *The Mirror Principle*

***

At about the same time that Alexander Bell was battling with family tragedy and relocating to Canada, Henry Ford was tending to his father's farm near Detroit, Michigan in the United States. There was one thing young Henry shared in common with Alexander Bell; he had a dream that was tied to his passion. His passion was for mechanical devices and how they worked. His dream was to own a company that made engines that were useful for daily endeavours. His father had hoped that Henry would take over the family farm, but Henry's passion for engines surpassed the lure of his obvious inheritance. At 15, Henry had gained a reputation for dismantling and reassembling machines as tiny as pocket watches with amazing accuracy.

At 16, Henry followed after his passions to work in the city of Detroit. He served as an apprentice for three years; spending his spare time to study machines at his place of work and how they were built. Even when he had to return back to aid his father on the farm, he studied the Westinghouse steam engine that was used on the farm and soon gained a job with Westinghouse Company to service their engines. Through this experience it became clear to Henry that people who have a genuine interest at a particular task tend to excel further than people who may have spent years working on the same thing but with a passing interest.

Buoyed on by nothing but his passion, Henry was employed as an engineer in the Edison Illuminating Company. In two years he was promoted to chief engineer. Incidentally the chief executive of the company was Thomas Edison, a great inventor himself. Seeing the spark for innovation in Henry, Thomas encouraged him to spend time on his automobile experiments. Another wealthy Detroit businessman, William Murphy believed in Ford's work and sponsored his first automobile company. Unfortunately customers perceived the cars made by Ford as too expensive and the company soon folded up.

Henry learnt vital lessons from that experience, and went on to found the Ford Motor Company producing more affordable models. His Model T car engines were unique and soon set the pace for engine design across the industry. It also introduced the car assembly lines for large-scale production. Within the next decade Henry Ford and his automobiles had become a force to reckon with in America. Today the Ford Motor Company is the second largest automobile maker in the United States and fifth largest in the world going by annual sales volume. The firm's global revenue in one year is in excess of 10 billion dollars and employs well over 150, 000 people around the world.

Henry Ford's life is a prime example of how The Mirror Principle provides success when its three simple conditions are met.

Sages Elixir

"Your time is limited so do not waste it living someone else's life. Do not let the voice of other people's opinion drown your own inner voice. Most importantly, have the courage to follow your heart and intuition. They

KJB

somehow already know what you truly want to become. Everything else is secondary"

Steve Jobs

***

In 1973 a boy was born to striving farm owners in the township of Asella in the Asri Province of Ethiopia. He was raised in a family of ten children. Like many children who grew up in the provincial areas of Africa, he had to face some cruel realities right from a tender age. Unlike many kids in our day today, he was not blessed with the luxury of hot and cold running water or a school bus to aid him to school. At just 12, he had to get up at early hours of the morning to help with the house chores until well after dawn. Then he would embark on a ten kilometre race to school; with his school books tucked underneath his left armpit. His name was Haile Gebrselassie.

As Haile made those dashes through the ill-kept roads of Ethiopia his mind began to dream. He dreamt of an estate well beyond the shores of his village. He had developed the gift of endurance. He wanted to be a long race champion. As he looked at the faces of the people he ran past each morning all he could think of was "one day I will be a champion, and I will earn enough money to improve the lives of my people". He admired the feats of a fellow countryman, Abebe Bikila and dreamt of achieving similar recognition.

Haile's passion for distance running was so great that he risked the wrath of his father so he could follow the finals of the 1980 Olympics 10km event on his father's cherished radio receiver. The batteries of the radio receiver were usually reserved only for news programmes but young Haile so badly wanted to be part of his much-loved event that a father's backlash was but a little threat.

With no professional training and at the age of 16, Haile took part in the famous Addis Ababa marathon and he excelled. Many took note of him and he was soon running for the police force. In spite of the meagre support that was offered to up and coming long distance runners at the time, Haile battled hard and pushed himself to remarkable limits. Galvanized by his dream to be a beacon of hope to his countrymen and a belief in his abilities, he toiled day and night. He pushed himself to go the extra mile where other runners called it a day or shut shop.

All the training paid off when Haile was picked to represent Ethiopia at the 1992 Junior World Championships in Seoul Korea. He won the 5km and 10km races. Dedicated to his goal, Haile went on to win the gold medal in the 10km event of the Atlanta Olympics at the age of 23. He has now broken sixty-one Ethiopian national records and twenty-seven world records. Till today, Haile Gebrselassie bears a signature posture when he runs. He still has his left arm crooked as though he is still holding those childhood school books; in those days of hardship that shaped his gift of endurance.

Haile's story is a reminder to us all that The Mirror Principle knows no boundaries. The Mirror Principle neither knows nor cares about your place of birth, gender, race, circumstances or intentions. Achievement only requires your dream, your potential and your mental focus.

***

Have you ever been so depressed that you contemplated ending your life? Not all of us have reached that point but we all have, at one moment in our lives or another, wondered if life is worth the hassle. Sometimes we go through phases when everything in our lives seem to be going wrong; times when every letter in the post or incoming phone call seems like another brick added to our load of misery. It is not those times that matter but it is our response in those times that make us who we are. Having the mental fortitude to face these stages of our lives is what defines us as champions.

This is yet another stirring story of someone who knows those distressing times all too well. Joanne had a passion for writing fictional stories and had taken to that passion from an early age. However at the age of 28, burdened with the need to fend for her baby daughter and the breakup of a marriage that lasted less than two years, Joanne was diagnosed with clinical depression. Indeed she had a dream to be a writer. She had started writing a few books but the darkness from the weight of her world blurred the vision of what she could achieve. One day nonetheless, she decided that she had listened to the sad press enough. She cleaned up the mirror image of her dreams and focused on what she could become.

While growing up Joanne had brushed up her writing skills by engaging herself with books with similar stories to the ones she dreamt of writing about. Her role model was Jessica Mitford, an acclaimed writer from Joanne's native country of England. From studying French at the University of Exeter to working in London as a researcher for Amnesty International, she kept scribbling down ideas for her fictional book. On a certain day, while on a delayed train trip between Manchester and London the idea of a story chronicling the adventures of an adolescent wizard flooded her mind. As soon as she arrived home Joanne rushed for her old typewriter and started writing.

Over the following four years she was faced with one ordeal after another. She lost her mother, suffered a failed marriage, and had a baby to look after without a proper job. She returned back to Scotland, and lived on state welfare support. She never stopped writing though; an evidence of determination. In spite of a busy schedule she would add a line or two to her book whenever she had a chance; sometimes in a café, or in any quiet place where her baby had managed to fall asleep.

After 5 years of writing, the book was ready. She submitted her manuscript to twelve different publishing houses and all twelve rejected it. Even when a small publishing house decided to publish Joanne's book, they advised her to get a proper job because they felt she had as much chance of making money from a children's book as nailing jelly to a tree. They were wrong. The story she told in her book was so enchanting that the demand for it exceeded expectations. Spurred on by the appreciation for her work Joanne wrote a few more sequels.

In the year 2000, less than three years after the first book was published, Joanne's series had broken world records, one of which was the fastest selling book ever. Her series have now sold 400 million copies and have been translated into sixty languages around the world. That fictional story which was conceived on a delayed train between Manchester and London, and started in a modest flat in London is the Harry Potter series. The woman who lived on social welfare, suffered from depression, and whose book twelve notable publishers rejected is none other than J K Rowling. Today Joanne's net worth is estimated at 1 billion US dollars. She was named as runner up in 2007 as Time Magazine's Person of the Year, and in 2010 she was voted as the most influential woman in Britain.

Let us make no mistake about it. Joanne was like very many of us. She was not born into a wealthy inheritance, or formally schooled in a prestigious college for literary arts. She had her own share of dark days, her years of doubts, and moments of anguish. J K Rowling would later describe poverty as "not having money to pay for a locksmith when your flat is broken into" or "contemplating shoplifting to get nappies" or "when your child is hungry but you are two pence short of a tin of baked beans". This was Joanne's reality at the time. Nonetheless she also had something else. She had a passion. She invested her mental energy into that passion, and kept her mirror image of who she could become right in front of her. The rest is now history as they say or better put, The Mirror Principle took care of the rest for her.

At a commencement address to Harvard students in 2008, Joanne relived the moments in her life where the dream seemed too far; reality was bleak and uninspiring. Today she describes failure as a stepping stone.

> *"Failure meant the stripping away of the inessential. I stopped pretending to myself that I was anything other*

than what I was, and began to direct all my energy to finishing the only work that mattered to me. Had I really succeeded at anything else, I might never have found the determination to succeed in the one area where I truly belonged. I was set free because my greatest fear had been realised and I was still alive; and I still had a daughter whom I adored; and I had an old typewriter and a big idea. And so rock bottom became a solid foundation upon which I rebuilt my life"

***

The Mirror Principle Works Even In The Tiny Details

It is not only in the huge achievements that we see The Mirror Principle in action. In little daily accomplishments we witness how the product of what we can do and our mental energy yields us results. The Mirror Principle works for short-term goals as much as it works for huge dreams and targets. Even for a goal as trivial as tidying up your house you require The Mirror Principle to complete it. Firstly you pictured the house in a tidier state. Secondly you were convinced that you had the ability within you to clean up the house. Thirdly you focused your thoughts and actions on putting things back in order. Soon the picture of a cleaner house became your reality. In just this simple accomplishment we see the mirror, the seed

The Mirror Principle

and the mind in action; your imagination, your ability and your focus respectively. The Mirror Principle is the law behind all human achievements; whether big or small; long term or short term; vague or specific.

Famous actor Tom Hanks once starred as a sole survivor of a plane crash. He was stranded on a lonely island in the movie Cast Away. The script had the trappings of an Oscar awardee and Tom Hanks knew this. In the plot, Tom plays a man on a routine business trip whose airplane loses its way in a violent storm. He is suddenly alone and forgotten on an Island. He lived on the island for four good years before he finally made it back to civilization. It was a story of courage; a moving tribute to the tenacity of the human spirit. The movie was a box office hit grossing over 400 million US dollars worldwide. Tom picked up a Golden Globe award and an Oscar nomination for Best Actor.

Tom's long term goal had been achieved. What may not have been obvious to many is that in order for him to achieve this end goal, other short-term goals had to be achieved. One of these short-term goals was to recreate the physical transformation of his character. Tom had to transform his physical appearance from a chubby middle-aged bloke to a hairy emaciated man during the course of producing the movie. This meant Tom had to first gain fifty pounds, and then lose over seventy pounds to be right for both parts. Tom set to the task by sticking to a very strict diet and endless workouts. There were times when he could have given up; but goal-getters never give in. As long as they can retain a mirror image of what they want to become, they devote their strengths to getting there.

The Mirror Principle Even in The Most Daring Missions

Christopher Reeves once said, "at first, all dreams seem impossible, then improbable and then inevitable". The world is replete with people who have used The Mirror Principle to overcome the most daunting of challenges. I dare say that one of the most difficult situations a person can face is embarking on a dream that the whole world believes is a fool's chase.

At the end of the 19th century, experts thought it was a waste of time to challenge the dynamics of gravity. The thought of a self-propelled, gravity-defying vehicle was insane. At about this same period, two brothers Wilbur and Orville Wright were investing their mental energies into creating this machine. Born with a passion for flying objects, the Wright brothers dreamt of a bird-like machine that could comfortably carry man for hours in the air.

The Mirror Principle

They studied flying kites and helicopter models in the backroom of a store in Dayton, Ohio. They locked themselves into the thoughts of building this machine. They studied the works of Sir George Cayley, Otto Lilienthal, Samson Langley and Leonardo Da Vinci who had published useful findings about aeronautical events. They believed that once they were able to combine an engine, a bird's wings and reliable control into one machine, the world's first airplane would be born. Amidst doubts and ridicule, they strove on. Every failed experiment only reinforced their belief that they were closer to achieving their goal. In December 1903, aided by nothing but sheer mental focus, the Wright brothers brought the airplane into reality.

In the same vein, just less than three hundred years ago many believed that the earth was flat. They said if anyone ventured to sail into waters not previously navigated, such a sail would encounter the edge of the earth and fall off. Christopher Columbus defied these odds and pictured continents on the other side. As he sojourned around the world, any doubts that still existed about the spherical shape of the earth soon evaporated. He charted new territories first in his mind's eye and they became a reality through dominant thought. His discoveries created shorter routes for travel and commerce.

Before 1954, the conventional wisdom was that human beings could not cover a mile in less than four minutes. Medical scientists said the human body could not be pushed beyond that limit. Roger Bannister broke this popular belief. He completed a one-mile race in less than four minutes. As soon as he disproved this notion, many more people have been encouraged to go on. Today there are thousands of people who finish the mile race in even less time.

Michelangelo was advised by experts that a certain kind of marble was worthless. Great sculptors like Agostino d'Antonio attempted to produce something out of this large piece of marble with little success. Michelangelo did not allow these failures to faze him. He held onto the rejected piece of marble. Then he focused on a mental image of a masterpiece that did not yet exist. He then set to his task; starting by roughening out the parts of the marble that were not part of the image he envisaged. The result of his skill and determination was David, one of the most revered sculptures on the planet; a seventeen feet long masterpiece once conceived in the mind of the artist but now a beautiful monument at the heart of human artistry.

Time after time we see records broken and feats achieved; achievements that were once believed to be humanly impossible. The Mirror Principle says that whatever the human mind can believe and strive towards, it can achieve. The Mirror

The Mirror Principle

Principle shows no bias towards the intentions of its achievers. This is why the most evil plan or selfish dream can be achieved using the same principle that has brought hope and joy to billions of people. As Time Magazine rightly opined in its defence of men it included in its list of the 100 most influential people "recognition of influence was based on the magnitude of impact whether the impact was for good or bad".

Whether the result is negative or positive, achievers held on to a mirror and used The Mirror Principle to achieve their results. Hitler had a mirror of a powerful leader who promotes extreme nationalist views and became exactly that using his skills of persuasion and oratory. Mahatma Gandhi had a mirror of an ideological leader and pioneer of nonviolent civil resistance. He used his gift of patience and intellectual sagacity to become this image. Mohammed Ali had a mirror image of a world heavyweight champion. Martin Luther King Jr. had a mirror of an advocate for civil rights in America. Nelson Mandela dreamt of the end of apartheid in his homeland. Bill Gates saw himself at the forefront of a computer revolution. Bill Clinton held a mirror of himself as President of the United States after meeting the charismatic John F. Kennedy in person at the age of seventeen. He followed it through with mental focus and the use of his charismatic skills; and he achieved his dreams. Edmund Hillary pictured himself on top of Mount Everest, and his mirror image soon became his reality.

The Mirror Principle Only Uses Ability; It is Blind to Disability

Many great courageous persons throughout history have proven that physical disability does not symbolise the end of the road. Even in disability there is ability. As long as the ability to imagine is kept alive, there are no bounds to what the mind can achieve.

Agatha Christie was a successful crime fiction writer. Not a lot of people know that she suffered from epilepsy all through her life. Beethoven lived with deafness while he composed and performed several groundbreaking musical pieces. He used special hearing tubes, and felt the vibrations of his piano to produce masterful compositions. Demosthenes had a passion for public speaking but had to overcome a stuttering impediment that he suffered from birth. He is today regarded as a leading light in the field of orations. Professor Stephen Hawking lived with cerebral palsy for almost all of his life. Although he was confined to a wheelchair, he defied these conditions to become a renowned physicist.

A Common Thread

When we take a close look at all the life examples we have recounted in this book we can see a common pattern. For instance we see that all achievements must face resistance. Dreams must be challenged by present realities that seek our attention. Another common trend is that the end goal usually stays the same, but the strategies used by these achievers tend to change through time and circumstances. In other words our mirror image for what we want to achieve stays the same but how we achieve our goal is ever changing.

Let us take the case of Henry Ford. He had to make changes to the model he envisioned when he realised that the model had some deficiencies. His end goal was to build automobiles much better than what previously existed. On the way to that end goal he had to revise his plans, change strategies and endure failure. Such is the nature of achievement. I might want to get from point A to B. I plan to get to point B by following a straight line. I soon realise that to get to my destination, I must sway several times to the right and then to the left. As long as my actions are driven by my end goal I could take these detours, but still make it to point B.

Some people erroneously think that changing strategies is a sign of lack of focus. This is not necessarily true. Lack of focus means changing your destination once faced with challenges. Lack of focus is changing your ultimate mirror image or your end goal from time to time. However, it is an act of brilliance to retain your end goal even while you realise that you need to take a different route to get there. Plans can change; strategies can be reviewed; short-term goals can be replaced. All that needs to stay unchanged when we use The Mirror Principle is our mirror image and mental focus. Plans change for various reasons. You might suddenly realise that there are complications on your journey that were not obvious at the beginning. Again you might realise that your knowledge on the subject matter has increased and with this knowledge comes a better strategy. In some cases other events have changed the way the world works and your plans change because you need to keep up with a new era.

Another truth that becomes evident as we look at the lives of achievers is that not all achievements bring you fulfilment. Only those achievements that are linked to your seed of purpose can bring you fulfilment. Even when some of these achievers succumbed to pressures and went on a different path, they always arrived at that point where mere achievement was not enough. They wanted fulfilment. Yes they did well at jobs that they felt less passionate about but until they came back to the one thing they were most passionate about,

The Mirror Principle

happiness eluded them. This goes to show that keeping true to your seed is equally as important as locating your seed. You may be good at many things but you are happiest doing what you were born to do.

We have said that every achiever maintains a mirror. What we probably need to also stress is that non-achievers have a mirror too. A man who sees a different image of himself everyday ends up with an obvious result: an unsteady and at best average life. His results are weak; his beliefs about his gifts are easily swayed by every wind of opinion; his works are suffocated by the circumstances he lets to overwhelm him. You are what you see in your mirror whether the image is great or not. A hopeless man sees limitations in his mirror. He allows past events and negative people to dominate his imagination. Rather than believe in lofty dreams he forms a thick wall of reasons why he will not make it. As he sees himself in that mirror, so he will become. Henry Ford was right in saying that "whether you think you can do it or not, you are right". You achieve what you believe. Our mirror is the reflection of our beliefs. Your mirror may be sketched by your imagination, but it is coloured and sustained by your beliefs. What do you believe about yourself? For what you believe is what you are bound to become. Ability gives you a chance; imagination gives you a destination; belief is what takes you there.

Perception is Reality

A famous experiment was performed on fleas. Scientists picked a flea for this experiment because it is known to jump extremely high. Fleas were kept in a jar for days. The jar was covered with a lid, but its height was far less than heights that fleas can normally attain. The fleas tried several times to jump beyond the lid of the jar. Each time, the fleas hit the lid of the jar; unable to go any further. Soon the fleas resigned to the fact that the height of the jar was unsurpassable. In their minds it was now futile to try jumping to heights beyond the lid. The fleas cautioned themselves to jump only close to the lid, and then drop back ensuring that they did not hit the lid. The scientists then took off the lid. Even then the fleas would not jump any higher. They would jump only to a height they had taught themselves to be the limit when the lid was there. So even though they had no limits, past experiences had dominated their beliefs. They had set an imaginary limit.

FACT

1. In a recent experiment, Piranhas were placed in a large tank but a glass barrier was placed between them and their food.

The Mirror Principle

Although they could see their food they were met with painful resistance anytime they tried to reach the food. Their heads kept crashing into the glass barrier and they could go no further. After a while the glass barrier was removed. By this time the piranhas had convinced themselves that there was no use in going for the food. The Piranhas starved to death although they were living in the midst of abundant food.

2. A baby elephant was found trapped in the bushes, entangled by a tough rope, and stuck to the base of a tree. The baby elephant tried unsuccessfully to break free, but after many attempts it resigned to its circumstance. Rescuers disentangled the elephant from the tree, but initially left the rope on the legs of the elephant. Interestingly, as long as the elephant saw the rope around its leg, it believed it was still trapped. If the elephant had moved away from the tree it would have realised all by itself that it was no longer bound to the tree. Nonetheless the repeated failed attempts and the sight of the rope limited the elephant to thoughts of captivity. The elephant only left the spot after the rope was taken off.

3. In 1963, Jane Elliott a school teacher, performed what is now known as the Blue-Eyes-Brown-Eyes experiment. Jane had told a class of school children that kids with blue

eyes were far more superior to kids with brown eyes. She told the kids that possessing blue eyes meant that they were far more intelligent and special than those with brown eyes. Within days of selling her message, Jane realised a profound change in the grades and behaviour of the students. The kids with blue eyes suddenly picked up on their confidence. They performed better on all the subjects they took. The kids with brown eyes slumped significantly. Even those brown-eyed kids who used to dominate the class dropped dramatically in grades and confidence. The scenario was reversed; the brown-eyed kids were coached on their superiority. The same trend was observed; the brown-eyed kids performed much better than the blue-eyed kids. Their beliefs dictated their image of themselves and eventually the results they attained.

Nature has been so kind to bless us with examples of milestones achieved by the power of belief. All of these milestones use The Mirror Principle. It may surprise you to know that the most powerful animal in the world in terms of body proportion is not the elephant, the lion or the bull. It is the rhinoceros beetle. It only reaches up to 3 inches in size but a rhinoceros beetle is able to lift weights that are 850 times its own weight. To put this in perspective, an elephant can only lift a quarter of its own weight. If humans were rhinoceros beetles we would easily lift a fully loaded passenger airplane; probably with a smile on our faces. It would have been utterly understandable if the rhinoceros beetle had looked at its size, and did not venture upon lifting such weights. To its credit, it looks at its ability rather than its disability. It believes that it can do it. Its perception of its ability has become its reality.

"Your Perception of Your Potential is Your Reality"
The Mirror Principle

One important aspect to touch upon as we look at The Mirror Principle in action is a concept I call the Mental Cyclic Effect. This refers to the interaction between the mind and the mirror. It illustrates the exchange that goes on between our self-image and our beliefs. There exists in us all a continuous exchange between who we think we are and what we do. Both sides affect each other. It is in our nature to believe in an image of ourselves; this image is what we see in our mirror. However, the same mirror turns back to affect our beliefs and hence our actions.

Let us say I have a passion for music and I have a dream to become a singer. I may set out with a mirror image of myself as a successful singer. Now that is great. If I go for several auditions and hear the feedback from music producers, they may paint a different picture for me about who I am. If I choose to believe something different from what my mirror says, very soon my mirror image will change to become the beliefs I now hold about myself. So we see a circular motion at the core of our achievements in life. This circular motion is the exchange between our imagination and our beliefs. Both would always seek to be in harmony with each other. Your goals suddenly become your belief. Then your beliefs soon dictate your goals.

The Mental Cyclic Effect is further evidence that our mind is nothing but mental energy. There are too many proofs to show that all energy is transferable including mental energy. Little wonder then that scientists have discovered that memory can be found in body organs. All things are made of energy and all energy interacts with each other. It is only when we look at things from this basic level that we understand how our minds work, and the wonderful things we can achieve just by knowing this.

As we look once more at the true life stories of The Mirror Principle in action, we see the importance of mental focus. Whatever we put our minds to do, as long as we have the potential within us to achieve, we will achieve. In the lives of Henry Ford, Alex Graham Bell, Haile Gebrselassie, Joanne K

The Mirror Principle

Rowling and many others we see living proof of how mental focus attracts supporters and tools that are instrumental to our success. Sometimes people come into our lives but we are unaware that we attracted them through our dominant thoughts and ultimately our actions.

Companies, countries and individuals use The Mirror Principle to chart their destinies. At the core of their past, present and future achievements is not only their ability but also their beliefs about that ability. Belief is a deep reservoir of mental energy, and it interacts with everything around us.

Sages Elixir

"Do not let your fire go out, spark by irreplaceable spark in the hopeless swaps of the not-quite, the not-yet, and the not-at-all. Do not let the hero in your soul perish in lonely frustration for the life you deserved and have never been able to reach. The world you desire can be won. It exists...it is real...it is possible...it's yours."

Ayn Rand

Nutshell

Your imagination, your ability and your focus: This combination is what drives your reality. Respectively they point to your mirror, your seed and your mind. Together they produce your reality.

Many talk about how they would love to change their circumstances. They say, "I wish I could improve my life". Well here is the truth: Your life is very much within your grasp; your circumstances are within your control. To change things you need to change your imagination, increase your focus and develop your ability.

It takes courage and hard work but there is a guarantee of success. The best guarantee you could ever get is one that is not made by men. The Mirror Principle is a natural law so it is not subservient to bias; nor is it subject to prejudice. Achievers in all fields of life have shown time and time again that The Mirror Principle is the most powerful determinant of human success.

6 Mirror Cleaners and Mirror Blurrers

There is nothing quite as important as the human mind in any endeavour. Your ability, your goals and your beliefs all reside in your mind. Your entire life is a product of your most dominant thoughts. This chapter is dedicated to those who have a purpose; those who know what makes them feel fulfilled; those who have the courage to live the life of their dreams. Once you have located your seed of purpose, and you have built the mirror image of what you want to become, this chapter shows you the practices to follow, and the practices to avoid.

These practices are vital because as earlier noted in this book, the mind is a battleground. Remember our analogy of the mind as a bare garden? The mind is the soil upon which your seed can grow into a beautiful garden. Like any soil your mind retains many different things; both the wanted and the unwanted. Your mind absorbs all kinds of information. The helpful bits of information help you to grow in stature and support your seed of purpose. The unhelpful bits of information are like foreign seeds, which eventually become weeds that attack your seed of purpose. Again just like any garden the more you entertain the weeds the more likely it is for your seed of purpose to be stifled. The seeds that flourish are those that are well attended to. Seeds that are left unattended may grow for a while but soon wither away. In the same light, potentials that we dedicate our minds to can flourish into achievements.

Sages Elixir

"Just as iron which is not used grows rusty and water putrefies and freezes in the cold, so the mind of which no use is made is spoilt"

Leonardo Da Vinci

"It is the mark of an educated mind to be able to entertain a thought without accepting it"

Aristotle

"Cultivation of the mind is as necessary as food to the body"

Cicero Marcus Tullius

The Mirror Principle

The mind is like a living room; a place where many decisions are taken. There are windows that give access to this living room. These windows are our five senses. They are the mind's link to the outside world. The senses of sight, hearing, smell, touch and taste are the windows of our minds. It is extremely important that we exert some control over the signals that these five senses send to our minds. Our mind relies on what these senses are communicating. Of these five senses, the senses of sight and hearing are two crucial windows that dictate the disposition of the mind. What we see and what we hear is vital.

Harry Houdini, a famous stuntman, performed one of the most fascinating stunts ever witnessed. Harry could make a large elephant disappear from the stage in front of a large audience. He had brilliantly mastered the Act of Misdirection. He like many who would come to find out the same concept, understood that the two crucial windows to controlling people's thoughts are the senses of sight and hearing. He was able to command the eyes and the ears of the audience. He enthralled them; he made them see and hear only that which he wanted them to see and hear. He did this so well that the next time the audience looked in the elephant's direction it had vanished and seemed to have disappeared from the stage. This act and many events in our everyday lives prove that our minds are at the mercy of our sight and hearing. Whatever the eye sees and the ear hears the mind believes.

Someone may argue saying "what about the blind and the deaf? How do they make up their minds if they cannot see or hear?" This assumption is an easy mistake to make; a misconception that those who are blind and deaf cannot see or hear. The fascinating truth is that sight and hearing are internal functions. Our eyes and ears may give us physical sights and sounds from the outside world but when either of these organs gets damaged we still have the power of sight and hearing. We may be physically blind but sight as far as the mind is concerned is the picture you see; your 'image in action' or imagination as we like to call it.

A blind woman might not see a physical car in front of her, but she can imagine it. As far as the mind is concerned, the car is what she is seeing. The same goes for a deaf man who is constantly hearing things within himself; even though he is not able to hear the sounds on the outside. He may not physically hear the sounds of the movie in a cinema but he can see the subtitles. These subtitles speak to him in sounds that the physical ear cannot pick up. So we see that we are all blessed with the capacity to see and hear.

The contents of our minds are hugely dependent on what we allow ourselves to see and hear. Our minds are the keys to our future, and the responsibility over our minds belongs to no one else but us. You can blame the government for your lack of education or blame your parents for your financial status, but you cannot hold anyone responsible for how you think or what you think about. This responsibility is fully yours. This fact may be a depressing reality for a lazy person, but it is the single most powerful tool for your fulfilment in life. To think that there are no limits to what our mind can achieve and that we are in control of our minds should be an uplifting message. Someone did rightly say, "life is a tragedy to those who feel, but a comedy to those who think".

Sages Elixir

"Tyrants have not yet discovered any chains that can keep the mind bound"

Charles Caleb Colton

"The moment the slave resolves that he will no longer be a slave, his fetters fall. Freedom and slavery are mental states"

Mahatma Gandhi

A study of The Mirror Principle in the lives of achievers and non-achievers alike equips us with the knowledge of the things that help us to attain our dreams, and things that kill our dreams. It sounds apropos to call them Mirror Cleaners and Mirror Blurrers. We all have a mirror in our minds; an image of ourselves that has the astonishing effect of transforming us into what we see. Once you have found your seed of purpose then you should create your mirror and keep looking into it. As you focus on the image in the mirror you are transformed into what you see.

Mirror Cleaners are forces that guide you to your mirror image. They are your helpers on your way to your happy destination. These are the practices you should embrace and encourage. On the other hand, Mirror Blurrers are forces that blur your vision. They attack the mirror image. If you invest your time and mental energy on them you will never get to that happy destination. With Mirror Blurrers you may get to a destination but it would not be your happy destination. Let us now elaborate on seven Mirror Cleaners and seven Mirror Blurrers, which help or deter us from the fulfilment of our ultimate goals.

Mirror Cleaners

1. Passion

Nothing sustains a dream quite like passion. It is the most natural mirror cleaner. It exudes from within and propels us like jet fuel. Our seeds of purpose come with immense passion. Whether it is singing, dancing, fashion, teaching, athletics, trading, public speaking, leadership, discovering, cooking, or inventing, our passions well up naturally from within us. Passion is excitement for what you do. Your mirror image should be tied to what you are naturally passionate about. It must make you want to get up from bed when others are lashing out at their alarm clocks in misery. You should do what you love and love what you do.

When you have passion for your goals there is a much greater chance that you will get to your destination. People who are passionate about their goals feel tremendous happiness when they go to work. What is more, they are most likely to put a better feel to their results. In every team endeavour the passionate people are easy to spot. Passion is so powerful that it does not hide itself. It is a strong form of mental energy released when we get involved in our lines of interest.

When we have passion for what we do we feel like we are in our comfort zone. As such we become more attractive. The magnetic energy, which exists in us all suddenly comes alive, and people are willing to listen to and follow us.

The reason passion is so powerful is because it is a genuine force. If it does not come naturally then it is as powerless as an inkless pen. Sometimes passionate people get criticized for being overly excited but the truth is nobody complains when they get promoted to the next level. Passion takes a cause forward, and in this world of so many misplaced priorities passionate people are easily spotted and promoted. When you have passion you work with a smile on your face and your thoughts flow better. It is like opening the window curtains to usher in a bright and lovely day. Passion is looking forward to what you do when you are away from it.

The fire of passion is so strong that it consumes the weeds that threaten our seed of purpose. When we turn on our passions our goal becomes clearer. It is as though the fire from our passion lights up our lives and we can see more clearly again. Passionate fire not only lights up our lives, it lights up the lives of the people around us. It is a release of energy that speaks to the chords of interest lying in others. Someone rightly remarked that "people may forget what you said but they will never forget how you made them feel". Our words, our actions and our works tend to take on the shape of our passions and people react accordingly.

Never fail to dance to the music that plays in your heart. It may not sound like music to the people around you but dance to it. It is the key to your happiness. You never know who would buy into your melody just because you gave life to the melody. Life has shown us countless examples of how the world danced to a melody that was once ignored. The fact that you hear a good melody that others do not hear does not make you useless. It may just mean that you were meant to lead the world in this new line of thought.

Sages Elixir

"The more intensely we feel about an idea or a goal the more assuredly the idea buried deep in our subconscious will direct us along the path to its fulfilment"

Earl Nightingale

Passion makes things happen for you, to you and because of you.

One great thing about passion is that it keeps you going when less passionate people feel the heat and bow out. You will face challenges on the way to your goal; these challenges are like strong winds. On the other hand, your passion could be likened to fire. Now here is how they relate: Strong winds put off small fires, but fan strong fires to flame. So it is with our passions. The strong wind of challenges puts off weak passions, but steers strong passions unto greater heights. If you do not have a strong love for what you do, discouragement could easily set in, and you will never be as productive as you need to be.

2. Potential

You can have all the passion in the world, but you must understand your potentials before you can achieve your goal. Your potential refers to your ability; your skills; things that you can do well. It is all good news around potential. One of such positive elements is that potential is a raw material that could always be improved upon. Potential is skill that can be made more beautiful; polished into finer forms.

Some people face a dilemma sometimes when they realise they are passionate about something they are not very skilful at. This is not a bad thing. You should not allow anyone to talk you out of your passions. To strive forward you could do one of two things. Firstly, you could apply yourself to make your skills better. Attend training courses and associate with people who possess such skillsets. After all, your natural passion would ensure that you learn faster and devote yourself to becoming better. Remember that there are some achievers who had a passion but their skills did not match up with their enthusiasm; they were laughed at when they first started out. Nonetheless, fired by their passion they applied themselves to learning and making themselves better. Sigmund Freud was booed from the stage when he first shared his scientific knowledge. Walt Disney was laid off by a newspaper editor for showing "a lack of imagination and good ideas". Marilyn Monroe was told her dreams were futile because "she was not pretty enough".

An alternative to the passion-skill imbalance is to work on something related to your passion. You could find that your potential lies in mentoring or supporting the key actors in your field. Let us assume that you love music. You could either aim to be a singer by training yourself for it, or you could become a songwriter, producer or promoter. The fact that you realise you have no potential for singing should not put you off your passion for music. The same goes for any other line of interest. It is no secret that the best coaches were not necessarily the greatest players in their time. Today we have some great sports coaches who could not compete as players. For these persons, their passion for the game has stayed intact; they understood their potentials and they harnessed it. They have stayed connected and relevant to the things they love.

So how is potential a Mirror Cleaner? Your talents give you hope; they remind you that you have what it takes to achieve your set goal. Every now and again, we get warm accolades and encouraging words about our talents. This positive feedback spurs us on to achieve more. There is also the inspiration that we get from past achievements. The laurels we have won and the short-term goals we have attained, no matter how small, serve as a signpost to the image we see in the mirror.

Sages Elixir

"Do not go where the path may lead, go instead where there is no path and leave a trail"

Ralph W. Emerson

3. A Plan

If anyone mocks you for being a dreamer or calls you an incurable optimist, you may win their hearts when you show them a realistic plan. If that does not win them over, then do not be dismayed. If you keep to the plan, they will soon turn from mockers to believers. Plans inject the substance of reality into our dreams. Whereas passion and potential give you the wings to fly, a plan gives you another important asset: direction. If your dreams could be likened to a galloping horse, then plans would be the reins that bring control. An effective plan should contain three parts, and we shall touch on each one in more detail.

The first facet a plan should have is the big picture. This is your mirror image. The picture of who you desire to become must be kept within your view as consistently as possible. Some people prefer to hold their plans mentally in their heads and that is great. The whole idea is to have it in your mind anyway. However for some reason that I am yet to fully understand, I do believe that penning down the big picture in a place where you can constantly view it or hear it has a profound effect on you. You may sketch it on a board, write it in a book, inscribe it on the wall, stick it on your bathroom mirror, stamp it on your desk, record it on a tape recorder, tattoo it on your palms, stick it to the fridge door; whatever you do just make it clear, heartfelt and always in your view. The idea behind this big picture is to flood your senses with the mirror image of your destination. This way your mind's dominant thought becomes the mirror image of your destination. It is essential that you keep the big picture in your view at all times. Many great accomplishments are a result of written goals. Great minds understand the need for a dressing mirror to appreciate physical beauty, but they value even more the mirror that shows them what they aim to become. Jim Carrey, before making a successful career in acting used to go about with a cheque in his pocket that he had written to himself and which said "Pay Jim Carrey ten million dollars for his acting services". Walt Disney had a rough sketch of Disneyland on his desk several years before he had the resources to explore his dream.

It may amaze you to realise the power generated by maintaining visual or audio compilations of your ultimate goal. There will surely be times when you feel like you have lost your way; or times when you do not feel fired up about your ultimate goal. At this time, the big picture comes in handy. It revitalizes you. You move from looking in that mirror to being inspired again. Remember that all things carry energy and energy is transferable. As you draw, speak or write down your dream, you transfer passionate energy into your mirror. At the time when you may feel down, if you gaze into your mirror it will send those energy signals right back to you. This is not superstitious talk. Science has and will continue to prove the substance behind the transference of energy.

Let us say you aspire to become a medical doctor. There is nothing wrong with putting this down on paper. You could write, "I am a medical doctor. I save lives and I am the best at what I do". You could even inscribe an image of a doctor in his lab coat with stethoscopes hanging down his neck. You could make a voice recording of what you have written, and save on your voice recorder. Every day you may wake up to look into that mirror, or read it aloud to yourself, or listen to the recording. You will be amazed to see the transformative power that these little routines bring into your life.

Sages Elixir

"Write down the vision and make it plain, so that he may run who reads it"

Habakkuk, The Prophet

Lord Byron did rightly say, "A drop of ink makes a million men think". Quite similar to a comment we have heard ever so many times that "the faintest ink is stronger than the greatest memory". What we capture on a physical material outside of our minds is easier to reproduce than the dreams we hold in the deep recesses of our thoughts.

The Reinforcers

Another extension to the big picture is having what I call Reinforcers. The big picture is like a motto, destination or vision statement. There are times when your mirror is not physically present with you. Sometimes you may not even be in the mood to look into the mirror. This is when reinforcers become useful on your way to your destination. Again the main idea behind reinforcers is to flood your senses and steer your mind into the right mood. Reinforcers give you renewed energy. Reinforcers use the powerful force of our emotions to remind us of the plan and why the plan is so worthwhile to us. If there is anything that aptly describes the common phrase "frame of mind" it is our emotional reinforcers. Like a frame for the mind, they hold the picture of our dreams firmly in place.

One of the greatest reinforcers in the world is music. As exposed in this book, our minds function by association. Music stirs up emotions in us that elevate us to higher grounds. It is often on these higher grounds that our dreams and passions exist. Make it a duty to surround yourself with music that connects you to your big picture. It is highly therapeutic and very effective. Like music, we may all testify to how a good movie, a theatre production, or most other forms of entertainment have a powerful influence on our moods. I personally have listened to certain songs or witnessed certain events that reinforced my plans in life. Never underestimate the power of music and other forms of media; they are effective reinforcers.

The Mirror Principle

FACT

1. A tailor-made music programme has been reported to reduce the need for pain relievers by up to fifty percent for thousands of patients. Scientists have used Auric Imaging to confirm that music can reduce pain, stress, depression, anger, fatigue and confusion.
2. Studies show that music could have a decisive influence on what you buy in a shop, or how much you spend when dining in a restaurant.
3. Haile Gebrselassie reportedly requested a techno song Scatman to be played on his way to winning an Olympic golden medal. Hurdler Moses Edwin listened to laid back soul music just before his over one hundred conquests on the tracks. Many renowned doctors are known to listen to classical music just before they enter into the surgical theatre.
4. Studies suggest that in a group where a small percentage of people write down their goals, success was more likely to be achieved by this small percentage than all others in the group.

There is a second facet to an effective plan: your short-term goals. Your short-term goals are very crucial to your progress on the road to realising your dream. Your big picture is a statement, but your short-term goals are your plan of action. You should have short-term goals that form a flight of stairs to your dream goal. These short-term goals must flow into each other. Short-term goals are much smaller than the dream goal. They could be specific and achievable within a short period of time. It does not matter if you have a thousand short-term goals that make up your ultimate goal, but you should always keep them clear and precise. Think of your big picture as a wall. Your short-term goals are the bricks you must lay, one on top of the other as you go along. If you take care of the little bricks the wall should take care of itself. You need the big plan to inspire you but the short-term plans represent each step you need to take. Every accomplishment of your short-term goals brings you a step closer to your achievements.

The third aspect to your plan is time. Time is perhaps man's most fleeting resource. We all have it, but we cannot control it. We can only control how we use it. It is one of those dear resources that get used up whether we make the best of it or not. Maya Angelou rightly commented that "time is the one immaterial object which we cannot influence; it is an imponderable valuable gift".

Time is of the essence. Hence your long and short-term goals should have timestamps all over them. If you want to be an architect you should have a timeline on when you hope to have accomplished this feat. A twenty-year-old woman who decides to become an architect could aim to get there at the age of thirty-five. In between now and her next fifteen years, she should then write down short-term goals like "attend college", "read up twenty good books on architecture", "work under a great architect for three years", and so on. Each of these short-term goals should also have a timeline.

The useful thing about using a plan is that you have the advantage of reinventing yourself from time to time. You could stop intermittently; bring out your plan and check to see how you are doing. This style of appraisal makes you assess how fast or slow you are going and where you may need to improve. Again plans could be used as a source of encouragement. A plan gives you the chance to look back and note your little achievements thus far. This gives you some fulfilment even though the whole task is not yet complete. Every short-term goal you realise gives you belief and satisfaction.

There is also nothing wrong with changing your short-term goals from time to time. In sports, the goal posts do not move about, but the route to get to the goal posts could change as you strive to reach them. It is better to have an unwavering ultimate goal and mirror image, but your strategies could change when you deem necessary. Like in the example of the architect we just mentioned, you may realise that working under a successful architect is not possible where you are located, so you could decide to read forty books instead of the twenty books you had earlier planned to read. Many seasoned coaches routinely tell their students, "Many roads lead to Rome". Destination is kept constant; route to destination can change.

Sages Elixir

"When it is obvious that the goals cannot be reached; do not adjust the goals; just adjust the action steps"

Confucius

4. Positive Company

We can never rule out the impact of other people's thoughts, words and actions on our lives. Unless you exist on an island all by yourself you are going to have people in your life. Some people you will interact with for only a moment in your lifetime; some will be around you for a while and then disappear; others will be around you for the long run. Your mirror is impacted by all these three sets of people. Some

The Mirror Principle

company are inevitable and a good example is your family. However the majority of our company are permitted into our circle of existence by virtue of where we go and the decisions we make.

The saying "show me your friends and I would tell you who you are" may seem clichéd but it is true. Your friends are the company you choose to keep. You may have met them accidentally, and you may not agree with the views of some of them but they are your company because you associate with them.

Now let me explain why company is so important. Again it goes back to the transference of energy. People send out different vibes. Humans and indeed all living things are constantly transmitting packets of energy. We are similar to routers; sending and receiving all kinds of signals. Whoever you are in the company of is actually interacting with you in more ways than you can imagine. Energy is forever in motion and looking to interact. This is why you can cheerfully walk into a room filled with so much sorrow and depression that your cheerfulness wears off. You may even take on the dominant energy yourself and assume a sad and despondent mood. For this reason, hospital patients tend to prefer some particular nurses to others. Those preferred nurses give off an energy that is comforting to these ill patients.

Now there is another aspect to company that we should realise. Some erroneously think that company simply means the people who you are physically surrounded by. Yes it means that and much more. Company also includes your interaction with the works of other people. For instance if you are presently in Stockholm and you are reading a book written by an author in New Zealand, through the transference of energy, you are in the company of the author even though he is not physically present. So a person might be long gone from this world, but we could be in their company when we interact with their works. Everything we do in our lives almost translates to keeping company. When we listen to music, watch people on television, read books or admire an artwork, we are keeping company with people.

Company transcends people. Animals and plants of all kinds are constantly interacting with us in ways unknown to our conscious minds. We are in much better states and our dreams are better protected when we understand the far reaching effects of company and strive to master it.

FACT

1. Neurophysiologists suggest that our limbic brain, which is responsible for our humanity and social interactions, operates like an open loop system. Hence a sizeable aspect of our personalities is created by our interactions with other living things that we come in contact with.
2. Researchers have once again corroborated the increasingly popular notion that couples tend to look and behave alike as they spend more time together.

Perhaps the best way of using company to our advantage is by viewing the company we keep as seeders. All company inadvertently drop seeds into our lives. Some seeds are good for our goals while some are not. It is our duty to determine which of these seeds are good or bad. Positive company sow seeds in your mind that encourage you to excel at your goals. Sometimes it might be just a pat on the back or a word of support but these nice little seeds are helpful. It is a wise thing to strive to be in the company of people who make you see your goals more clearly; people who fill you with hope. Good books, pets, movies, music, events and many more could also make for positive company.

5. Role models and mentors

Knowing someone who has accomplished his or her goals is always a refreshing advantage. The spirit of success is like a ripple on a water surface. It reverberates far; it reminds you that goals are achievable. To maintain a clear mirror image, you should flood yourself with as many success stories as you can fetch. Moreover, you should learn to see success in as many things as you possibly can. Nothing stimulates the goal setter more than another testimony of accomplished goals.

It is a good thing to have role models; people who embody qualities that you would like to have. Role models make you know that your goals are attainable because they are humans like you. Surround yourself with biographies or stories of your role models. Soon the challenges they faced and their reactions to those challenges will become real to you. You could learn how to avoid the mistakes they made and annex their strengths. The hindsight of your role models may prevent the injuries of your foresight. Strive also to be in touch with them. They may have specific advice to render to you for your specific goal. Resources spent on gleaning counsel, or associating with your role model, are never wasted; they are always an investment into your fulfilment.

Mentors are also important Mirror Cleaners. They act as life coaches to us. In many cases our mentors may not have achieved the kind of goals that we see in our mirror but their experiences in life help us avoid life's many pitfalls. Mentors do not have to be as passionate or as successful as we are but they are people of character; persons who are not afraid to look at us in the eyes and tell us the truth. Our mentors show us our faults and work with us to overcome them. Your role model might not even know you but mentors are willing to sacrifice their time and resources so you could be all you were born to be.

Whether they are our parents, teachers, spouses or bosses, our true mentors always want the best for us. They know us perhaps more than anybody else. Even at times when we may disagree with them we should never be fooled into thinking that they do not wish the best for us. Use your mentors and ask them questions. Allow them to appraise your plans and repay their trust when you have an opportunity to do so.

6. Helping others

The success of others is vital to your own success. More so if you work in a team, or your goal is tied to the success of a group of people. Even if your goal is an individual one, you will need and meet people along the path to your fulfilment. Nothing could help you more than working with a group of successful people.

Sometimes as humans we tend to indulge in the wrong attitudes towards success. One of these attitudes is jealousy. Thoughts like "Oh! I cannot believe he got the results I have been aiming for" or "Great! Just when I thought I could clinch the last chunk of success, now she has got it" or "why did it happen to her and not me" are common thoughts but they represent the wrong attitudes to success. Jealousy is born out of a wrong mentality. I call it The Scarcity Mentality. It is the mentality that says, "there is not enough to go around". Many wrongly think that success is a VIP box with limited seats. This is a hopeless man's fallacy. The truth is that there is always enough to go round everybody. Nobody can take your own success away from you. To think that there are limited seats for success signifies a lack of character and imagination. We shall touch more on this on the latter pages of this book.

Make it a point of duty to appreciate and work towards other people's success, no matter whom they are. The easiest way to imbibe this mentality without being jealous is to be aware of your own uniqueness. Secondly, you should acknowledge that the best habit to have is to complement, and not to compete with other people. Make it clear to yourself that you are only in a competition with yourself. To compete with others is to live a life of limitation; thinking life throws only one prize to one winner. When you understand that opportunities are endless you shall find a certain fulfilment in supporting other people's needs.

Does spending time to help others impact negatively on the time you need to fulfil your goals? The truthful answer is no. In fact if anything it speeds you up on your road to achievement. As an employee in a corporate environment it struck me to observe that certain persons who helped others the most tended to achieve more. I have tried to analyse this and one reason I could come up with is that people generally are eager to help these particular persons because they know these persons always offer a genuine helping hand to them. Again still on this note, how many times have we pondered at a certain task of our own? Then we took a break to help someone else with their own challenge only for us to realise, while helping someone else, we discovered the answers to our own questions.

Sages Elixir

"The first question which the priests and the Levite asked was "if I stop to help this man, what might happen to me?". But the Good Samaritan reversed the

question *"if I do not stop to help this man, what will happen to him?""*

Martin L King Jr.

"Thousands of candles can be lighted from a single candle. And the light of that candle will not be shortened. Happiness is never decreased by being shared"

Buddha

7. Adversity

There are many who would frown at the mention of adversity on the venerable list of Mirror Cleaners. After all, adversity does mean a "state of serious or continued difficulty or misfortune". From time immemorial all great achievers have agreed on this one thing; that adversity is useful on the road to achievement.

Sages Elixir

"What seems to us as bitter trials are often blessings in disguise"

Oscar Wilde

The Mirror Principle

To reach your goal you have to learn to welcome adversity. You could use adversities to your advantage. Whether they come in the form of the death of a loved one, loss of a mentor, illness, failure, bankruptcy, criminal attack, natural disaster, open persecution, unfavourable government policy, or an accident, adversities could become effective Mirror Cleaners. Challenges often come to you to give your achievements even more substance. Always look away from what you lost through adversity. Focus your mind on the good things that the travail brought to you. There is always something positive to gain from the furnace of adversity.

Adversity takes your potential to the next level. As you face a challenge the experience builds your character. It stretches your potential, and in stretching, you attain a new height. In truth the problems you face are the catalysts for your growth. Only those who do not understand this concept fall at the feet of their problems or retreat from the beautiful race they once started. Failures are quitters, but the wise person never gives up on a goal. I once heard a doctor say, "every problem tends to gravitate towards its own solution". Sometimes the solution to our problem lies within the problem itself. Little wonder then that vaccines, the celebrated defences against diseases, are made from the very same organisms that cause those diseases. Achievers would tell you that challenges are the burning furnace where their raw skills were refined into the rare gems that have dazzled the world.

Winston Churchill was revered as an orator although he was born a stutterer. He took great effort in mastering his speeches and the extra effort gave him an edge when he spoke. Another born stutterer was the man widely acclaimed as the most eloquent orator that ever lived; the man called Demosthenes. James Earl Jones, Bruce Willis and Isaac Newton all used the same adversity to their advantage in their careers.

Alexander Bell battled with a lifelong illness. Helen Keller was deaf and dumb. Walt Disney started several failed companies. Henry Ford lived through bankruptcy. Abraham Lincoln suffered numerous defeats and could not win a notable election until he gave the presidency a shot. Thomas Edison failed with the light bulb invention over a thousand times. J K Rowling battled depression. The list is endless. For these past and present heroes their passions soared like a kite; the contrary winds of adversity only urged them higher.

Another benefit of adversity is that it gives you a new perspective to things. Sometimes our minds are so stuck on a certain idea, or a trusted way to reach our goal. In some cases nothing changes until an adverse event knocks us off our perch. As we recover from that adversity we suddenly realise that there was an easier or a better way to meet the target.

Sometimes we become too comfortable with past achievements; it takes adversity to wake us up from our slumber so we can get going again.

The Mirror Blurrers

1. Past Failure

Remember a few pages back we talked about the stories of the fleas, the baby elephant, and the piranhas. They tried many times but they resigned. They all had goals. As they tried they were met with failure that made them turn their backs on their goals. They all had one thing in common; they let past failures convince them that their dreams were unachievable. For each failure they suffered, they shed another claw and loosened their grip on their dreams. True achievers pick themselves up from failure, but losers stay defeated and unprepared to try again. A past failure could be a Mirror Blurrer if it makes you see impossibilities rather than new possibilities.

Some experts do say that the meaning of insanity is doing the same thing over and over again and expecting a different result. This is generally true but there is an exception to this rule. It is called gainful persistence. There are some achievements that require sustained action. Picture a nail that you need to hammer into a strong concrete wall. At the first few strikes it may appear as though the wall is not going to budge. Yet after persistent strikes to the nail, the wall gives in, and the nail drills into the wall. Some goals require some level of persistence. To back down at the first few strikes is to give up too early. This is why you may find someone who claims that nailing on that wall is a waste of time, while someone else has proved him wrong through persistence.

The art of intelligence is knowing when to be persistent and when to devise a new plan. Notice here that turning back is not an option. When faced with the ghost of past failures you should decide whether to try again or devise a new strategy. The wrong thing to do is to turn your back on your dream.

Sages Elixir

"It is not the critic who counts; not the man who points out how the strong man stumbles, or where the doer of deeds could have done them better. The credit belongs to the man who is actually in the arena, whose face is marred by dust and sweat and blood, who strives valiantly; who errs and comes short again and again; because there is not effort without error and shortcomings; but who does actually strive to do the deed; who knows the great enthusiasm, the great devotion,

who spends himself in a worthy cause, who at the best knows in the end the triumph of high achievement and who at the worst, if he fails, at least he fails while daring greatly. So that his place shall never be with those cold and timid souls who know neither victory nor defeat."

Theodore Roosevelt

2. Addictions

Some of us have suffered them; all of us know someone whose life has been ruined by them; the stubborn demons of addiction. An addiction is a habit that we are enslaved to; a practice that we crave to indulge in even at our own peril. Addictions, in the context of this book can be defined as things we indulge in at the expense of positive goals in our lives. Addictions are as varied as they are destructive. Most addictions stem from the abnormal use of privileges or substances. Everything has a purpose but when purpose is unknown abuse is inevitable. As the name suggests, Abuse means ABnormal USE. Alcohol, money, power, sex, food, and drugs could all become our addiction.

Again using our garden analogy, addictions are best described as weeds. They are constantly fighting for more attention for themselves, which means less attention to your seed of purpose. The subtle way addictions blur the mirror image is by occupying your time, mental energy, and resources. Just like the gardener and his plants, the more encouragement you give to the weeds of your addictions the more powerful they become; conversely the less powerful your seed of purpose becomes. Addictions are your distractions in life. In my life I have met a fair share of very talented men and women who cannot put their talents to good use because they are bound by addictions. We have also witnessed millions of success stories that crumbled under the weight of addictions.

The reason addictions are so powerful is because they are our passions. They excite us and hence they ensnare us. They give us temporary pleasure but permanent pain. Addictions give us a false sense of hope; soon we find ourselves under their control. We then spend our precious time either indulging them or looking forward to our next fix. First we invite them into our lives, and then like a wicked guest they rule our lives. They leave us with no time, and ensure that the only time we get is spent in worshipping them.

Does this mean that having passion for our goals is also an addiction? No. There is a huge difference between passion and obsession. Addiction is an obsession. Obsessions make no room for rational thought; they are destructive and they add no value to your dreams. True passion is enriching and not destructive. One effective way of dealing with your addictions is to give your goals more value; polish your dreams to be more attractive to you. When you add more value to your goals you soon realise that these addictions interfere with things you cherish. Slowly, you would begin to spend time and resources on the right things.

We could even be addicted to our own success. There is a danger in spending too much time adoring your own achievements. This tends to create a comfort zone that becomes quite difficult to get out of. Suddenly you realise that you have lost the zeal to carry on; simply because you got obsessed by what you have achieved. Someone once rightly said, "the reward for a job well done is the opportunity to do more". There is always more to accomplish; more seas to conquer; more horizons to discover. Strive to be the best you can possibly be.

If you presently suffer from an addiction, it is not too late. Be resolute about dealing with it. Take it for what it is; a destructive habit. Like weeds these addictions are stubborn and must be dug out right from the roots.

3. Fears and Doubts

If addictions are the weeds in our garden of dreams then fears and doubts are the rocks that stop our seeds from growing. Like rocks hiding deep in the soil we must dig them out and get rid of them. When we leave fears and doubts in our minds, our seed of purpose is inhibited from growing.

Let us say you have a goal to become a renowned tailor. You step out into your dream, but you suddenly realise there are thousands of tailors with a clientele firmly held under their grip. It appears to you that your potential customers already have so many options to choose from. Then you begin to doubt your success. You think, "there are too many good tailors out there". Then you look in the newspaper, and all you hear is how bad the economy is. You fear that you may never have enough capital to make your move. In both cases you may be wrong. There is always room for more and the economy is never bad for everybody all the time. This is what achievers prove every day.

Fears and doubts present you with impossibilities. They corrupt the vision of your dreams with thoughts that are sometimes very rational. With these formidable thoughts, we are faced with reasons why we cannot progress so much so that we forget the reasons why we can. The proven way to conquer our doubts and fears is to face them. There is a motto that seems to eliminate them; a phrase of three words: Just Do It. All human beings encounter fears and doubts but it is this motto that sets the achievers from the rest of the pack. Achievers like to focus on the why not's rather than the why's; the possibilities rather than the limitations. It is as simple as that. Our fears are often reasonable; doubts are often natural. Yet the only way to overcome them is to go ahead with the task and just do it. It is alright to slip into thinking of these limitations, but you should shake these limiting thoughts off by focusing your mental energy on performing the task at hand.

You will not discover new oceans unless you have the courage to leave the shores. You would only complain and convince yourself of a thousand reasons why you cannot make it across the ocean unless you make an effort. How many times have we taken a bold step only to find out that all the limitations were not as formidable as we thought? As we come out with courage we suddenly realise that our limitations were not real. Most of the reasons we expect to make us fail are not real. They are only a figment of our imagination. Yet we let them stop us from taking the needed step. Even in the unlikely event of failure, we are better off with the knowledge we gained from the experience. This result is much better when compared to doing nothing at all.

Anytime you are faced with certain fears or doubts, remind yourself that you would never be walking about today if you had never dared to stop crawling as a child. You will never discover new oceans if you are too afraid to lose sight of the shores. Think of the many things you do now that you would never have done if you were too afraid to engage them. Doubts and fears are thoughts; thoughts carry tremendous energy. Hence it is true that when you doubt your power you give power to your doubts.

Sages Elixir

"No one can make you feel inferior without your consent"

"Do the thing that you fear the most and the death of fear is certain"

Mark Twain

Remember when faced with fears and doubts, Just Do It.

4. Money

Many would be surprised to see money named as a Mirror Blurrer. "Money answers all things", one might argue. Yes there is some truth in that. Money is an immensely powerful tool. Money gives you the power to perform; the impetus to acquire anything that could be bought. However, it is for this very same reason that money is on the list of Mirror Blurrers. There are so many ways of getting money. It could help you obtain many things; it opens many doors. Whether you are in South America or North Africa; Asia or Europe; in a town or city; young or old; you need money to survive. The more of it you possess the bigger opportunities you could potentially have. Money is almost next to oxygen in terms of means of survival in today's world. It is the sheer pressure to acquire money that makes it a potential Mirror Blurrer. Strikingly money is often the source of our greatest frustrations.

Let us not lay a wrong benchmark though. Money is a useful tool when we understand its place in our lives. Like all good things, it is when we misunderstand its purpose that it becomes a Mirror Blurrer in our lives. We need to understand the concept of money and then master it. Failure to do so could inflict one of the greatest frustrations ever known to man. So it is not money itself that is a Mirror Blurrer; it is our conception of it. Of all the dream-killers money has the most devastating effect on us; it forces us to have the wrong priorities and then keeps us bound and leaves us unhappy. Money is a foe to those who fear it but a friend to those who master it.

How you spend money does not make you a master of it; this merely means that you are a wise spender. On the other hand, being miserly does not make you a master of money. On the contrary, it shows you are a slave to it. What makes you a master of money is how you acquire it. You are only a master of money when you acquire it for doing something you love to do. This assertion shall be explained.

Money is an invention of man but the need for it is as old as man. Throughout man's existence we have had needs. This is just the way we are; we have needs. When one person is convinced that he needs something that another person has, he inevitably must provide something of equal value in exchange for the thing he needs. Rewind back to five thousand years ago when there were no dollar bills, Yen or the Pound Sterling. Our forefathers had needs. To satisfy their needs they gave from whatever they had in abundance to someone who needed what they had, and had what they needed. So if my great grandfather needed a measure of grain he would give something of value, maybe a small farm animal, to someone who had the measure of grain. Today we do not need to trade by barter. The concept of money is now predominantly in paper currency. This paper currency is assigned different values by the government. This way we can trade without looking for someone that wants exactly what we have. I can imagine our forefathers must have felt very frustrated when they had so many cattle but not enough grain sellers interested in their cattle for exchange. Paper currency was invented to make trading easier, but the concept of money has not changed.

Now this is where the short history trip was headed: Money is simply a paper symbol for wealth. Wealth is internal; it lies within. Wealth lies inside of us. When people need the wealth we have they are willing to let go of their money to enjoy from that wealth. I hope you get the point. It might help to go through the last few lines again to let that thought sink in. Money is only a symbol of wealth, and wealth lies within us.

Let us look at a brief illustration of the role that money plays in our lives. There are two men both aged twenty. One is Mr Dee and the other is Mr Kay. They are both located in the same place. Each has very little money and a gift in sculpting. Mr Dee decides that he would stick to what he loves to do. He invests his little money into sculpting classes. His passion becomes obvious to his teachers; they are strong admirers but they do not have the funds to sponsor his works. Although he chooses to work four hours a day as a bartender to support himself, he returns back to his modest apartment every night to engage in the sculpting he loves. After six years his works get noticed and he is soon contracted by agencies who want to buy his works. In a few years, still doing what he loves, Mr. Dee is living very comfortably indeed. He works for himself and has a huge clientele from government circles to wealthy individuals.

Mr Kay on the other hand was also born to be a great sculptor. He also invests his little money into sculpting classes. Soon he realises that sculpting is not the most popular profession. The money he may earn from sculpting might not bring him the prosperous life that he desires. He soon starts a family that he needs to support. He branches off into banking. Relying on his natural brilliance, Mr Kay makes a career out of banking. Although he knows within himself that his true passion is sculpting, his need for money drives him away from his passion. He is more driven towards staying afloat. He succeeds in keeping up with the Joneses and lives the life of a successful banker.

At age forty-five, we revisit the lives of both men. Both have achieved success at their jobs. Both of them are financially comfortable. This however is where the semblance ends. One man is completely independent, healthier, less stressed and most importantly, he feels fulfilled. The other is depressed because he has no time to do what he loves. His unhappiness rubs off on those around him. He probably needs to work for another twenty years before he could retire. In essence, money was a Mirror Cleaner to one man and a Mirror Blurrer to the other.

The above illustration depicts the lives of many people. It is important we understand the concept of money early enough in our lives. This knowledge prevents money from killing our dreams. It might suffice to add that not many people who go the money-making route even end up becoming successful. Many struggle until their last days on earth; they live for the next drop of money. Meanwhile on the other side of the fence, a few people are enjoying every minute of their lives. They are doing what they were born to do and money is taking its normal place in their lives. In the lives of achievers money has no choice. Money serves those who invest in the wealth within. Fulfilled people know that wealth lies within. They bring forth their wealth and it is inevitable that people are willing to give up their money to be in receipt of these persons' wealth.

Do not aim to be rich. Just aim to meet a need with the wealth you have within. An old fable reads "Fools dream of riches; the wise dream of happiness". Quite true. Plan your life around that which makes you happy. Money has a way of taking care of itself. There are countless numbers of rich people who testify that most of the money they have made has come unknowingly to them; as they went about doing something that they were passionate about.

> **Sages Elixir**
> *"You can only become truly accomplished at something you love. Do not make money your goal. Instead pursue the things you love doing and then do them so well that people can not take their eyes off of you"*
>
> Maya Angelou

5. Negative Company

We have probably overused the analogy of the mind as soil, and your dreams as a garden. We said the potential, which produces this garden, is your seed. Doubts and fears are like the rocks in the soil. Addictions are like weeds that compete for our resources. In this same context, negative company are the rodents and pests that lurk around; seeking to destroy your seed as it tries to grow. Rodents and pests see no point in a seed's growth. The same is true for negative company.

The Mirror Principle

Earlier on we took a deeper look at the meaning of company and how company inevitably affects us. Negative company always tries to push us away from our goals. Whether the company is in the form of family, friends, television programs, books, music or other forms of media, the goal of negative company is to pull you further away from achieving your goal.

So how do you know if you are keeping negative company? The litmus test for company is to list the people, things and forms of media that you spend your time with. Think back to the normal days in your recent past. Who and what have you spent the hours of your life with? From the time you got out of bed until you went to sleep, who and what did you spend time with? Make a list of this. Start from the ones you spent the most time with to the ones you spent the least time with. Then list out the value of each of these companies. Value is based on the worth each company adds to you in terms of achieving your goal. I call it the Company WatchList.

Let us look at a practical example. We look at the lives of two normal people with similar ambitions. Both lists show two people who keep roughly the same kind of company over fourteen hours of their day. The difference between the two is that each person allotted different amounts of time with each company. At the end of the day it is easy to see why one person succeeds beautifully at his goal but the other does not.

Name of Person 1: Mr Kay
Goal – To become a grocery shop owner
Company WatchList

	Company	Offering	Time Spent	Value in Minutes	Value in Percentage
1	Newspaper	He reads the pages of economic gloom	30 mins	0 mins	0%
2	Magazine	He settles on gossip that is unrelated to his goal	30 mins	3 mins	10%
3	Passionate Friends	Positive encouragement and useful suggestions	30 mins	30 mins	100%
4	Gym	Relaxation and good health	1 hour	45 mins	75%
5	Self-Help Book	Strategies on how to succeed in business by a famous author	30 mins	30 mins	100%
6	Drinking Buddies	Banter	4 hours	18 mins	10%
7	Despondent People	Fear; negative experiences, stories of hopeless situations	3 hours	0	0%
8	TV	Settles for uninspiring channels	3 hours	9 mins	5%
9	Social Networks	Settles for gossip, banter and pranks	2 hours	6 mins	5%
	TOTAL		14 hrs (840 mins)	141 mins	17%

Name of Person 2: Mr Dee
Goal – To become a grocery shop owner
Company WatchList

	Company	Offering	Time Spent	Value in Minutes	Value in Percentage
1	Newspaper	He reads the pages that inspire him	30 mins	22.5 mins	75%
2	Magazine	He settles on stories that are related to his goal	30 mins	22.5 mins	75%
3	Passionate Friends	Positive encouragement and useful suggestions	3 hours	180 mins	100%
4	Gym	Relaxation and good health	1 hour	45 mins	75%
5	Self-Help Book	Strategies on how to succeed in business by a famous author	2 hours	120 mins	100%
6	Drinking Buddies	Banter	1 hour	6 mins	10%
7	Despondent People	Fear; negative experiences, stories of hopeless situations	1 hour	0	0%
8	TV	Settles for inspiring programs	3 hours	135 mins	75%
9	Social Networks	Settles for networking with useful friends, family and mentors	2 hours	90 mins	75%
	TOTAL		14 hrs (840 mins)	621 mins	74%

This straightforward statistic shows an astonishing difference. It shows the value that each person gets from the same kind of company by virtue of the time they devote to each company. Mr Kay could only wish for the things that Mr Dee will achieve. This is because Mr Dee has chosen to surround himself with the right company. As you consciously analyse the company you keep you soon realise that some add little value; some add good value while others devalue your dreams.

Your true friends should add value to your goals, and would support you to achieve them. On the other hand, people who do not care about their goals, rarely care about anybody else's. Once you bring these people into your life, one of two things happen. You either become their positive company, or they become your negative company. When you sense that a certain company is taking you away from your goals it may be the time for you to give less time to such company. Remember too that misery loves company. As negative people drown deeper in despair they tend to feel better by pulling everyone down along with them.

You should aim to always be a positive company; and be surrounded by positive company. It is vital that you do not descend to the estate of miserable people; whose small minds make mockery of ideas, and only revel in gossip or misfortune.

Negative people tend to dwell on their disadvantages. Some resign themselves to merely discussing the lives of other people; they fail to trust in their own dreams. It is a sign of laziness to constantly discuss about people when you have an unlimited bank of potential at your disposal.

Sages Elixir

"Small minds discuss people. Average minds discuss events. Great minds discuss ideas."

Eleanor Roosevelt

"A true friend knows your weaknesses but shows you your strengths; feels your fears but fortifies your faith; sees your anxieties but frees your spirit; recognizes your disabilities but emphasizes your possibilities."

Williams A. Ward

6. Wrong Experts

One of the most daunting Mirror Blurrers is an expert. Our society needs experts. They are men and women with tremendous insight into their fields. Experts are people of vast experience who have proven themselves in their fields of endeavour. Many of them have used The Mirror Principle to climb out of the shackles of insignificance; they now sit at the prime echelons of their fields. Once the status of expert is attained, a person becomes an authority in that discipline. Titles could be bought but experts always earn their place through dedication to a cause.

Experts are trusted for their knowledge. Their words become laws that govern their field of expertise. Any aspiring person in any discipline of life must learn by the rules of these experts. They are our role models, lawmakers, teachers and statesmen. However, experts are human and sometimes, though not very often, experts could be wrong. Many experts have a downside to them; they hate to be wrong. It is at this point, where the conception of something new threatens the foundations of established knowledge that experts become Mirror Blurrers.

While it is wise to learn and seek counsel from experts, you should realise that your best guide on your road to fulfilment is your intuition. Your intuition is that inner voice in your heart; the voice of hope and innocence; it is the closest thing to your seed of purpose so trust it. It is important to follow established routes for the most part of your journey. Nonetheless we should never cow under the pressure of experts, and in doing so, fail to express ourselves. Remember that every law or design that is in place today had to face the scrutiny of the authorities of the day. They earned their place by proving their worth to a sceptical audience. It is only rational for people to trust standing rules rather than experiment with something new. This is the reason why achievers are celebrated; they are courageous souls who faced the odds but pressed onward. They were not deterred by an established order because they believed in their potential.

Sages Elixir

"The future belongs to those who believe in the beauty of their dreams"

Eleanor Roosevelt

"Believe nothing, no matter where you read it, or who said it, no matter if I have said it, unless it agrees with your own reason and your own common sense."

Buddha

Thomas Edison was labelled as "unproductive" by his first boss. His teachers said he was too stupid to learn anything. Beethoven was warned by a music teacher never to venture into composing music because he was not good enough in this area. Stephen King wrote Carrie, the bestselling classic that became so successful that it enjoyed film and TV adaptations.

The same book suffered rejection from thirty publishers who thought the story had no place in the bookstores. The Warner brothers first rejected the idea of movies with sounds when it was first proposed. "Who in the world wants to hear actors talk?" was their first response. This occurred as recently as 1927. A renowned record label told the Beatles that their sounds were outdated, and that music with guitars was fast fading.

Technology companies rejected Steve Jobs' ideas of a personal computer. One of these companies said Steve had no college degree, and wanted to have nothing to do with his ideas. Twenty big companies between 1939 and 1944 all rejected the initiative of Chester Carlson when he proposed the idea of a photocopy machine. To every expert he approached, the mocking question was "Who would ever want to copy a document on plain paper?" Meryl Streep is an Oscar winner and leading actress in Hollywood. When she first started out, a renowned film producer was infuriated when Meryl came on stage to audition for a role in the movie 'King Kong'. "She is ugly. Why did you bring me this thing?" he asked in annoyance. There is also Damien Hirst who was refused admission into the Leeds College of Arts because he had an E grade in Art when he took his A-levels. Today Damien Hirst is one of Britain's most celebrated artists.

All these rejections did not come from mere negative people; they came from the authorities of the day. The experts were wrong; they failed to see beyond the norm; they could not discern the next big thing. Just because they are experts in a particular field does not always mean that they will be the first to see a better way to do things in their fields. Their wealth of experience is not a guarantee that they will appreciate your seed of purpose.

7. Impatience

There is a story about a farmer who went to his field to plant seeds. The seeds grew into little plants and the farmer was pleased. Suddenly the plants began to wither and they looked poorly. The farmer noticed they lacked water. He watered the plants more frequently and they began to blossom again. Now he wanted quick results. In a bid to see them blossom even further the farmer watered the plants even more. In a short while the plants died; they were flooded with too much water. The simple lesson here is "never allow impatience to kill your dream". The Mirror Principle is a natural law. Natural laws do not happen overnight. They move at a pace and act alongside other natural laws. You should appreciate this about your goals as you strive to meet them.

The Mirror Principle

On your way to fulfilment there will be times that require you to wait. No matter how passionate or gifted you are, there are times when things come to a standstill. The reason for this is that there are other forces that work for your success; these forces all work at different paces. As an aspiring athlete you may have trained vigorously and prepared yourself but you cannot determine the day of your race. You may have to wait for it. Soldiers have to wait for commands to engage; farmers have to wait for planting season; parents have to wait on their kids to learn; chickens have to wait for their eggs to hatch. Waiting is an unavoidable experience in our lives.

When you give in to the pressures that come with waiting, you let the cloud of impatience blur your mirror image. With a blurred vision, you may likely step out on the wrong foot. There is a time for everything. A time to sow and a time to reap; a time to be born and a time to die; a time to rejoice and a time to mourn; a time to start and a time to stop.

So the question is what do you do while you wait? There are two valuable things you could do. You could either prepare yourself for the road ahead, or simply get some rest.

As the Boy Scouts would tell you, there is no such thing as over-preparation. Whilst you wait to be called onto the stage it helps to retrieve your script and practice. Go over the plan.

You may be amazed how much more firepower you pick up when you wait for the next big thing on your journey.

Perhaps the most effective thing to do while you wait is to rest. Yes, take a break. Sometimes we could get so passionate about our dreams that it consumes us to a point where we forget the value of rest. Rest is vital to any success. In your plans for achievement, you will do yourself a world of good to set aside ample time to rest.

True achievers understand the value of rest. It tackles the menace of impatience that haunts passionate people. Taking time off from doing the thing you love means you have time to enjoy other things you want to do. Partaking in these side activities refreshes you. After a rest you come back on to your business like a recharged battery. As you involve yourself in other activities, your comprehension broadens. Imbibing a rest culture is embracing one of the finest arts of life: The Art of Balance. Every achievement can only be sustained through the art of balance. When one part of our lives suffers we are prone to make the wrong decisions. If you love your family and friends, you should learn to devote time to them. They often come back to support you on your journey.

Plan to take holidays from time to time. If you are unable to travel away, at least take breaks. Studies have proven that the more you focus on a task without taking breaks, the less productive you become. Try to keep your eye on the ball, but you should try to spoil yourself sometimes. Resting is a powerful therapy. A person who spends an uninterrupted twenty-four hours trying to solve a problem may not achieve as much as a person who works at it for the same length of time but takes breaks.

Sages Elixir

"Every now and then, go away. Have a little relaxation; for when you come back to your work your judgement will be surer"

Leonardo Da Vinci

"He that can take rest is greater than he that can take cities"

Benjamin Franklin

Nutshell

Every year we celebrate the lives of brave soldiers; men and women of courage who risk their lives to defend the noble ideals of our nations. Without these brave souls our world could be overrun by tyrants.

There is another person whose efforts of courage we sometimes overlook. That person is you. You have fought thousands of wars that you may not even know about. You are a soldier but you may not even know it. All your life, you have been drawn into the battlefield of the mind. The mind is a combat zone where thoughts fight for supremacy. An average human being is exposed to thousands of thoughts each day. The decision on which thoughts we yield to is totally in our hands. For every day you stay sane and decide not to wreck your life or the life of others, you win yet another battle in your mind.

We are quick to castigate the world's criminals, mass murderers and scoundrels. Only doctors who have worked with these criminals would describe them as people who have lost the war of mental balance. We see them as dangerous predators but they are actually victims of mental disorders. They have lost their minds to perverse thoughts; their backbones have been broken; they have succumbed to evil.

If you have not reached this breaking point; if in spite of the challenges and pressures of life you have stayed sane and positive, then you deserve some tribute. Every day you have engaged with others thoughts in the battlefield of your mind. You maintained the resolve to keep going. Every fellow human should appreciate your feats as a soldier; just as you should appreciate theirs.

There is a higher level of success to attain on the mind's battlefield. It is winning the battle of purpose. It is finding and focusing on your purpose amidst all other thoughts. It is success at this battle that sets the achievers from the non-achievers; the extraordinary from the ordinary; the fulfilled from the unfulfilled.

If you would keep your passion alive and dance to the music that plays in your heart; if you would nurture your potential like you would nurture your own baby; if you would place the vision right before your eyes and break it into short-term goals; if you would surround yourself with positive people; if you would listen to the counsel of your mentors but dare to challenge the established knowledge of experts; if you would meet with adversity holding the belief that harsh times only make you better; if you believe that helping others is as beneficial as helping yourself; if you can see past the disappointments of failure; if you can resist the vain passions that have ruined many gifted people; if you can doubt your doubts and face your fears; if you understand that money is only a paper symbol for the wealth within; and if you master the art of resting while you wait; you shall meet with your dreams even at unexpected hours.

7 The Mirror Principle And An Organization

We have spent some time looking at the effects of The Mirror Principle in individual lives. Now we take a close look at The Mirror Principle in the life of an organization.

An organization refers to any group of people who work together to achieve a collective goal. An organization could be set up for profit, as is the case with many businesses; for public service, as is the case with government institutions; for non-profit service, as is the case with charities; amongst other reasons. Whatever the purpose an organisation is set up for, it is certain to involve more than one individual.

An organisation at its best is stronger than any one individual because it stands on the combined effort of more than one individual. A popular proverb says that "one will chase a thousand; two will chase ten thousand". One of the first lessons I learnt in life was the strength in unity. I was given a simple task at the time. I was handed a single stick and asked to try and break it. I did this rather easily. Then I was handed a bunch of the same sticks; the sticks were fastened together into a sizeable bunch. Breaking the bunch was impossible. I struggled with it for an eternity, and the bunch would not break. In that simple lesson I had learnt to appreciate the strength in a group; the power of unity.

Our world runs on organisations. There are as many industries as there are facets of life. Each industry supports a sector of human life. It is mind-blowing when we pause to consider the number of fields of industry that exist in today's world. It almost makes you wonder why anyone could feel hopeless or pessimistic. There are indeed millions of fields out there for anyone to get into and make their mark. When you talk about industries or jobs most people immediately limit their minds to the obvious careers like legal practice, medicine, banking, telecoms, media, engineering, the family business, and a few others. It pays to see further than this. It pays to see the vast amount of opportunities that exist in other endeavours in our world.

FACT

1. There are over seven billion people on the planet. That means there are over seven billion potential consumers out

there. A good example to illustrate this is the recently revealed cell phone statistics. In 1985, there were only a few hundred cell phone users across the world. In 2010, the number of cell phones in circulation was over 4.5 billion.

2. A recent study went to some length to disprove the notion of population explosion, pointing out that the popular view that the world's population is expanding too rapidly for earth's resources to sustain us might be an overly pessimistic notion. One of the evaluations that the study undertook was on the availability of land. The study revealed that only one city in the United States, the city of Jacksonville in Florida, contains 84 square miles or 23.4 billion square feet of land. At a world population of 7.5 billion, if you allocate a space of roughly 3 square feet to each person, all the people of the world would stand shoulder to shoulder, and still not fully occupy the city limits of Jacksonville, Florida.

3. Studies show that the presence of alarming poverty, famines, and depravity, in some parts of the world is a result of improper distribution of resources; not a lack of resources. 27 percent (close to one third) of the food in developed countries is wasted. Meanwhile over 1 billion

people in the world lack good food. Strikingly, the same number of people are overweight and struggle with obesity.
4. Half of America owns less than 1 percent of America's stocks and bonds but an elite one percent owns more than 50 percent. Statistics show that the poorest 40 percent in the world control a tiny 5 percent of world income. The richest 1 percent of the world population control over 40 percent of global income.
5. There are over 2.5 million technology companies in the world. Technology is only one of the thousands of industries that exist. When we add non-profit organizations and government institutions the number of organizations worldwide could pass the amazing 1 billion mark.

It is a world of opportunities if we open our minds to the bright truth. How often we forget that someone out there made the chairs we are sitting on, or the desks in our homes and offices. Someone made the computers that the traders need to survive. Someone made the clothes you are wearing; and we can delve even deeper. Someone made the labels, the fabric, the threads, and the machines that the clothing lines used to make the clothes you are putting on. Somebody somewhere makes millions of dollars making the bolts and nuts which are used to build the engines which are used to move the cranes which are used to build the skyscrapers which are used to house the traders that run the world's economy. These traders make profits; but so do the builders of their workplaces and apartments; and likewise the cleaning agencies who maintain the building; and the makers of the solution that the cleaners use; and the researchers of the chemicals that are used to make the solutions. The world is a mighty web of organizations.

Businesses and other organizations are springing up every day. On the other hand some are folding up. Some organizations succeed for centuries while some others never hit the ground running. At the heart of all organizations is The Mirror Principle. Whether it is a profit or non-profit, huge or small organization, The Mirror Principle determines its level of success.

"Your Perception of Your Potential is Your Reality"
The Mirror Principle

Every organization is under the inevitable influence of The Mirror Principle. The stock market may determine your net worth; government policies may affect your strategy; but there is something that underlines your success in your field: it is

The Mirror Principle

your market share. Your market share is the volume of activity in your industry that is directly controlled by your product, service, or brand. Your market share indicates your prominence in your field. The Mirror Principle to a very large extent determines your market share, and consequently your success as an organization.

There are some organizations whose goal is not to be the leading service provider in their field; their only goal is to be a participant. This is a very meaningful goal, and The Mirror Principle still determines whether you reach that goal or not.

So whether the goal is to be the best in your industry or to be a part of the industry, The Mirror Principle could be used to your advantage. It is wise to leave the financial strategies to the financial experts, and the management strategies to the trained managers. Nonetheless the overall success of an organization rises and falls on The Mirror Principle.

The seed, the mirror and the mind form the tripod stand upon which all human success stands. We shall take a look at the essential structure of an organization, and discuss how The Mirror Principle operates within these structures. We shall recognize classic examples of successful organizations that have used The Mirror Principle to their benefit. We shall also take a look at some unsuccessful stories that failed to use The Mirror Principle to their advantage. This chapter could be useful to start-ups, existing businesses that are looking to reinvent themselves, and to those organizations that are already successful but want to continue being successful.

The Seed Of The Organization

On earlier pages we found out that the seed pre-exists everything. We also stated that a seed is the proof of the existence of a need. Your seeds point to your ideas, your passion, or your potentials. They say necessity is the mother of invention, and I cannot agree more. When organizations are set up in response to gaping holes in our society these organizations tend to thrive. It is almost as if there is a natural market waiting to consume your potential.

Many set out to form an organization without even thinking if the organization is needed. Sometimes they have a good product and target market, but they fail to assess the market to see if it needs their product. In today's world you cannot impose your product on people. If you attempt this they will resist you. The best way to establish your product in the market is to build the product around people's needs. People respond to and will pay for products that they are convinced they need.

The Mirror Principle

People are usually persuaded by their needs; not by imposition. I once read one of Aesop's fables. It illustrates the success of persuasion over force. The great north wind challenged the sun to a competition. "Which of the two of us can make a passing traveller take off his cloak?" the north wind challenged. "I bet it is me", it boasted. The sun obliged to the contest. The north wind went first. It blew hard on the traveller. However the harder it blew the more the traveller held on to his cloak and wrapped it together against himself. Then the sun had a go. It warmed up the place slowly. Soon the traveller began to feel the heat. As the sun shone brighter the traveller realised he would feel better with his cloak off. He did just that. The sun had won. The lesson of this fable was: People resist force, but they yield to their needs.

In 1998 a former securities lawyer, Peter Thiel, witnessed the rise of eBay's online transaction volumes. He saw the need for a secure software system to facilitate electronic transfer of payments. This need gave birth to PayPal. Within four years of its start-up PayPal was valued at 1.5 billion US Dollars.

So someone says, "Well I already have my own organization and we are pretty successful. Do I need to hunt for more needs?" The answer is yes. It is one thing to be successful, and a different thing to sustain that success. To maintain your relevance you have to keep looking to meet people's ever evolving needs. At the turn of the millennium, Blockbuster Inc. was the leading company in home video and video game rental. The company had large stores where customers could walk in and rent movies and games. They were smart enough to move with technology from VCRs to CDs and then DVDs, but when people started desiring home deliveries the company failed to respond. Soon the needs of their customers turned towards online entertainment and cable on demand. Other outfits like Netflix, iTunes and cable on demand latched in on these opportunities. Today Blockbuster Inc. is now history. Its failure emphasized the benefits of staying in touch with people's needs. To this end customer feedback is hugely important. Whether they are present or potential customers, it is profitable to take on board their reviews about your product or service.

Another vital aspect of your seed as an organization is research. To strengthen your ideas or goals, invest your time into research. This is one investment that duly fetches its rewards. The best farmers are those who understand their seeds. The most successful software developers spend the most part of their time studying requirements before they venture into the act of coding. Leading companies spend huge amounts of resources on research before they launch new products. Research gives root to your seeds before they emerge on the surface. The deeper the roots the more likely the plant will survive. Political campaign organizations ideally set up an exploration team first before the campaign train is set in motion. Your research will help you absorb any potential shocks you may encounter on the way to achieving your goal. Research makes you aware of the dangers beforehand. The words of Abraham Lincoln rightly capture this. He said, "if you give me six hours to chop down a tree, I will spend the first four hours in sharpening the axe".

A third and equally vital aspect of your seed as an organization is your potential. The potential of an organization is the sum total of the potential of its members. When you start up a firm you may soon realise that you do not possess all the potential required to run the firm. So you bring in persons with the needed skillsets to partner with you. The potential in an organization is only as good as the potential of the people employed in the organization. For a new organization, recruiting is vital. For an existing organization, recruiting should always be a top priority. If the recruiting process has gone wrong over time, it may be time to restructure. People make an organisation what it is. Hence you should restructure anytime one or more of the four essential groups of personnel are lacking within the organization.

The four essential groups of personnel are: The Researchers, The Deliverers, The Marketers and The Managers. Every organization needs them in different proportions but you need them all the same. Your structure and idea could be unique to you but your potential is increased if you have these four essential groups represented in your organization.

The Researchers

These are your analysts; your deep thinkers. In a sense they play devil's advocate to an idea. Their intent is not to kill the idea but to test it. They subject any idea to a rigorous refinement process. They take the idea from its raw state of idealism to a more robust level of feasibility. Researchers help you to understand your exposures. Hence they show you signs of incompetence early enough for you to curtail them. Firstly, they help you figure out who your target market should be. Then like doctors they check the pulse of the market; they acquaint you with the directions that the markets are going. They are your eyes and ears. They keep you updated with the times.

The Mirror Principle

The Marketers

Perception is reality. A product is only as good as it is perceived to be. Your organization, whether it is a business or non-profit one, has a product or service it intends to sell to achieve a goal. This product could be a charity, a new technology, or a million other possibilities. You need people who are gifted in the art of selling to help you sell. These are your marketers. They understand the power of sensory perception. They know that whatever the eye sees and the ear hears the mind believes. Marketers possess the uncanny ability to make your target audience aware of their own needs; and how your product can meet these needs.

Marketers create your brand. They project an image of your organization to the outside world. All your good work will not matter if your organization is not viewed with credibility. This makes your image crucial to your growth. You should strive to project an image of credibility because as a wise woman once succinctly put it, "your credibility is your best currency". In so doing you must speak honestly of your product and emphasize its strengths. Leave this skill in the hands of your marketers. This group of people understand that the mind works by association. They are able to attach your product to the things we love. Good marketers know the product. They understand the need to be credible. They draw connections between the product and people's needs.

The Deliverers

The deliverers are the engine of the organization. They ensure that the product is created to a prescribed standard. They are the people who get their hands dirty on the production line. They take the product from the design phase into physical reality. If your organization were a restaurant, your deliverers would range from the actual cooks to the waiters and cleaners. They create the substance behind the product. As the product makers they know the standards of the organization and they strive to maintain it.

Deliverers should have the skills required in the field to which your products belong. If your organization produces automobiles, your deliverers will not be medical doctors or baseball players. Rather they would likely be engineers and physicists. It is crucial to also get the best out of these people. These people are skilled; they turn your idea from a dream into physical reality. You should strive to bring the best of them into your organization and keep them. The best amongst them tend to deliver with high levels of accuracy and speed, which improves the credibility of your product.

The Mirror Principle

The Managers

These are your leaders and project managers. They think, live and feed on the plan. They are planners. They bring direction and structure to the organization. They may not be skilled in marketing or make the best deliverers, but their talent is priceless. They have the extraordinary ability of knowing the right things to do at the right time. In any organization there will always be a million and one ways to do things. You will be faced with options and knife-edged decisions. The managers are employed to make these decisions. The good managers make the right decisions almost always.

Managers are usually much fewer in number than researchers, deliverers and marketers but they direct the other three groups on where to go. They also map out a plan; a roadmap to your destination. Their job is to make sure that the organization does not lose sight of the plan. Managers are leaders. They must be well informed, brave and fair. This way they inspire the confidence of those they lead.

The Mirror Of The Organization

So now you have a well-researched idea. You have also recruited talented people to study, promote, deliver and manage your product. However, to take your organization from potential to fulfilment the members all need to know what your organization considers as its fulfilment.

As people come to your organization, they have different ideas of what fulfilment means. Their different backgrounds and orientations mean they see things differently. If an organization ventures any further without having a consensus agreement on its definition of fulfilment, sooner or later, the organization would end up scattered like ash on a windy terrain. It is for this reason that the mirror becomes perhaps the most vital asset of any organization. The mirror is your vision statement. It is you in the next two, ten, or fifty years. Your mirror is the image of where you want to be. It is the image of your success.

Your mirror provides a rallying point for your organization. It is the vision set down for a group of people. It presents one vision to your team. An organization without a clear mirror opens itself to division. Division means diverse visions (Di-Vision). Division is a cancer to any organization. Division breeds confusion, strife and unhealthy competition. The Mirror Principle still works where there is division. It acts on the diverse visions and carries everyone in different directions. Everyone ends up bumping into each other until the organization implodes. The mirror brings stability and a sense of direction when it is properly used.

The mirror forms the central feature of this book. We earlier talked about its almost mystical ability. Many may have relegated the mirror's usage to physical beauty checks in our bedrooms, but its power must never be underestimated. The ancients revered the transformative power of mirrors, and it is still very much a part of our lives. The Mirror Principle works as a natural law in our lives. Only a few people take advantage of it, and use it to attain the one thing we all seek: fulfilment. If an organization does not have a clear vision it may accidentally succeed but it will not sustain that success. The question every group should ask themselves is "how do you know you have succeeded when you do not know the benchmark for your success?" How do employees strive for a goal they do not know? Remember that to know it, they have to see it.

On earlier pages we discovered that what people actually see is not what they see with their physical eyes. People see what their mind's eye communicates to them; the pictures created by their visual perception or sense of sight. The same applies to hearing. So in order for the people in an organization to know the goal, it has to find its way into their minds through their eyes and ears. They need to be able to visualize the vision.

They all need to know the dreams of the organization, and have a clear picture of where you are going as a group. It is the mirror that shows them this image. The Mirror Principle allows individuals and groups to create their own image. All it demands is that you keep your eyes focused on that image. The transformative power of the mirror ensures that you become what you steadfastly see.

Great organizations have a mirror. They ensure that their employees are constantly looking into that mirror. Your group should have a clear and inspiring vision statement. What do you want to become? Who do you want to be? These answers should be the image that everyone within your organization sees. Avaya is a leader in world communications systems and services. Its mirror says, "We provide the world's best communications solutions that enable businesses to excel". When automobile parts supplier Dana Corporation started in 1904 its mirror was, "I am growing profitable in the world's vehicular markets. I provide leading shareholder value and I find ways to make cars more fuel efficient". Today Dana Corporation is a Fortune 500 company renowned for their alternative fuel-powered engines.

The Dow Chemical Company says "I am essential to human progress by mastering science and technology". MetLife Inc is the largest producer of life insurance in America.

The Mirror Principle

It says on its mirror, "I aim to make all my customers met for life. I balance the efficiencies of new technologies with the personal touch of highly trained professionals and I deliver solutions that exceed my customers' expectations. This way I earn their loyalty". Facebook says "I give people the power to share, and make the world more open and connected". Google's mirror says "I organize the world's information and make it universally accessible and useful". For YouTube the mirror image it sees is "a provider of easy video access, and the ability to share videos frequently". Doctors Without Borders see themselves "delivering emergency aid to people affected by armed conflicts, epidemics, exclusion from healthcare, natural and man-made disasters in more than seventy countries".

All of these successful organizations have used The Mirror Principle to their advantage. At the centre of their success is a mirror image they have created by themselves. Perhaps more importantly, they have successfully enshrined the image in the minds of their employees. The battle for success as an organization is won and lost in the minds of your employees. To achieve the right results you should strive to have a place in the minds of your employees. The researchers, marketers, deliverers and managers should all be focused on the same image. The key to achieving this is to flood their senses with this image. Human beings need constant reminders of who they are; hence the need for the constant use of a mirror. Until the vision becomes a part of their own mental image, you should continue to flood their minds with these constant reminders.

Earlier on these pages we talked about reinforcers. They are ever so important in forging the right image into the minds of those who make up your organization. Reinforcers subtly make people breathe, live and love the dream. Successful organizations spend valuable resources creating these subtle reminders. Plaques around the workplace, meaningful logos, mission and vision statements as PC screensavers, workshops, seminars, and stickers bearing the vision statement may sound trivial but have a profound effect on an organization's productivity. These reinforcers are like paint brushes; they paint an image of a common aspiration. It is true that many Google employees prefer to wear their Google inscribed T-shirts to the office; it steadies their mind on the company's goal.

A common mistake that organizations tend to make is that they create their mirror image around the works of their competitors. They set out by looking at the goals of others. They build their image solely around replicating or bettering the success of others. Truly successful organizations concentrate less on their competitors and more on their own

The Mirror Principle

ability when they create their mirrors. This gives their product a feel of uniqueness that sets them above the others. Apple Inc. is a prime illustration of this truth. When Apple sets its targets, it is not merely reacting to the innovations and products of its competitors. Instead, it focuses on the power of its own ideas. It works towards bringing the best out of its own ideas. A quick glance at the iPhone, iPad, Mac PCs and the iPod shows that Apple looked within itself, and produced devices that the world found irresistible. It could easily have set its sights on bettering the stereotypical devices of the day but Apple focused on its internal vision. Apple, like many truly successful organizations, does not react to its external rivals. Rather it responds to its internal goals. If any organization could strive to be the best that they can be, they may not need to bother very much about their competitors.

Understanding Competition

If I go on the streets and randomly ask ten people to describe their views on the term 'competition' I am very likely going to have over two thirds of them describe it this way: Competition means fighting for a place that other people are interested in getting into. It is the act of contesting for a prize that yourself and another is interested in.

This outlook on competition is not healthy. The notion that 'outdoing a fellow human being is a mark of excellence' threatens our claims to having more civility than other mere animals. For so long we have based our fulfilment on how we have performed in relation to our peers, neighbours or siblings. Human beings naturally want to have a benchmark to assess their success, and these benchmarks are good to have. However, seeking fulfilment at the expense of other people's failure is not the right way to achieve success. Competition is a good thing, but true competition is not against an external rival; it is working on yourself to meet your internal goals.

The reason people and organizations tend to compete the wrong way is because they go about their business with the wrong mentality. I call it the Scarcity Mentality. It is the mentality that there are never enough resources, and that there is only one winner in any scenario. They look at the vacancy ads on a newspaper, and they see only one role up for grabs. The questions they fail to ask themselves is "Whatever happened to creating a new role? Who says that the employer could not be convinced to take more on board? In fact, who says you cannot create a niche for yourself outside of what is immediately available?" It all comes down to one thing: The use of imagination. When people or organizations restrict their imaginative ability they slowly edge towards a scarcity mentality, and they are forced to view competition as a duel to outdo their rivals.

As we saw from the Apple example, true achievers look inward and compete with their set targets. Humans, and by extension organizations, are so equipped with the power to create that they are capable of creating new markets and better products in any field irrespective of the economic situation. Life is not a rat race; it should be a celebration of creativity. Winning is not outdoing a fellow human being; it is achieving your set targets. Being the best does not mean you are better than others; it simply means you have made the best of the potentials you have within you.

Sages Elixir

"If a man would write a better book, preach a better sermon, or make a better mousetrap than his neighbour, though he builds his house in the woods, the world will make a beaten path to his door"

Ralph W. Emerson

When you have a clear vision statement it becomes easier to have a plan. The managers of your organization are then able to put a project plan together. The end result of the project plan is the mirror image that you have created. We discussed the importance of long and short-term plans under Mirror Cleaners. You could also leverage a clear vision in building a structure for your organization. With your goals in mind you could structure your resources in a way that best suits your goal. How many deliverers should you have? How much marketing does your product require? How many researchers do you need? Should you have several layers of managers, or a star-shaped leadership strategy? All these questions around your structure are best answered after a clear vision statement has been achieved.

The Mind Of The Organization

Every organization has a mind. The minute the leader of an organization begins to view the mind of the organization as a single entity the leader discovers a perspective that is capable of taking the organization to a much higher height. Indeed an organization should be viewed as a person; an individual with a goal. This person has got a brain, mental energy, can talk, see, listen and imagine. From this perspective we deduce the concept of the mind of an organization. Each employee is a vital organ; an essential part of the whole body. A pain felt by one organ could also be felt throughout the organization. A loss incurred by one organ could impact the entire organization. Psychologists attest to this concept; some call it the singularity concept; many people coming together to form a singular entity.

The Mirror Principle works in your favour if the people in your organization are of one mind. Organizations that have achieved success could only do so as a result of oneness of purpose. The more unity there is in the objectives of the various parts, the more success the whole entity would enjoy. This is common knowledge. A house that revolts against itself never stands. On the positive side, when people agree to work together towards a shared goal, the power created by the harmony of their thoughts is almost unstoppable.

There are many things you could underestimate in life; there are a few that should never be underestimated. One of such phenomena that should never be taken lightly is what some sages have called "The Spirit of The Mob". Never underestimate the Spirit of The Mob. It is a huge force. Put in simple terms, The Spirit of The Mob is the coming together of human minds. Hopefully in earlier chapters you have realised the inherent power in the mental energy of a single human being. When two or more human beings come together, and mentally agree to achieve one goal, the energy released as a result of their union is almost immeasurable. If this combined mental energy is sustained there is no telling where its impact could reach.

Some observers have noted that there could be a fifth element capable of bringing everything on earth to its knees. Traditionally there are four known elements whose force, when unleashed, could have the most telling effects on our world. The four elements are Water, Wind, Fire and Earth. The fifth element that some observers are now studying with curiosity is The Spirit of The Mob; the combined mental energy of unified thought.

Let us see a brief example of how the spirit of the mob works. Again it is a lesson in the transference of energy. If you follow any sport where games are played on a home-and-away basis, you may have asked the question "Why is winning a home game considered easier than winning an away game?" In other words why is the team playing at home regarded as having an advantage? After all, the pitches they play on are almost all the same? Sports commentators call it the home advantage. The answer is not farfetched. The advantage lies in the crowd of fans. The home team usually has more people cheering them on from the stands. By simply urging their team on, these people have formed a synergy of mental energy directed towards their beloved team. The players on the pitch obviously have the same desire as their fans to win. They are spurred on, not only by their individual energy but also by the momentum generated by the crowd.

So this phenomenon which commentators call the home advantage is a simple example of the Spirit of The Mob. You only need to have witnessed a public demonstration of some sorts before you realise how enormous the spirit of the mob could become. I have witnessed entire cities brought down because of public outrage. Some social analysts have tried to explain it. Everyone has huge reservoirs of pent up emotions neatly stashed under their social appearance. If an incident triggers these emotions, and if several people share that emotion at the same time and in the same place, these people could release a combined energy so strong that it leads them to do incredible things. This energy leads them to do things collectively; things that they could never have done individually. If you take a sincere look into your life, you may recall times when you did something based on a prevailing emotion. On your own you may never have done it, but there was a crowd of people thinking the exact same thought. In the heat of the crowd's behaviour you acted. In these moments you released energy at the same frequency with the crowd, and the combined force created a mob that then takes control of everyone including you. You were connected to the spirit of the mob.

The truth about the spirit of the mob is that it can only affect people of the same minds. If there is a crowd of people all thinking the same thought someone with a different mindset may not get involved. When the people in your organization have oneness of mind, an outsider would quickly notice what they might call "the culture of your organization". There is a prevailing mindset in every organization. This is why it is important to nurture that mindset. First you want oneness of mind in your organization. Next you want oneness in the right direction. Ensure to maintain a collective and positive mindset across your organization.

The best organizations are built on teams with a collective mentality to succeed as an organization. They have the right attitudes. There is an exciting feeling about their objectives. Everyone recognizes their contribution to the overall success, and they engage their mental energy to accomplish the vision. This is the reason why the recruiting process is crucial; you need to get passionate people into your group; people who will genuinely press on with the goals of the organization. Dedication should come naturally. Therefore it is beneficial to work with people whose dreams and passions in life tie into your dreams as an organization.

The first believers in your product should be your team. If there is enough passion within your group, your consumers tend to feel the passion when they come in contact with your products. It is often better to have a small team of passionate and united minds than to have a large group of uninterested people working for you. The synergy and positivity they produce is vital to the success of the organization. Observe an orchestra for instance. The beauty of an orchestra is in the harmony of all the players. From the violinist to the snare drummer and to the piano player, everyone is playing from the same script. At the end of the day the result is a beautiful symphony often greeted with satisfaction and applause.

Sages Elixir

"What is a drop of rain, compared to the storm? What is a thought, compared to the mind? Our unity is full of wonder which your tiny individualism cannot even conceive."

Ken Levine

Whether you fail or succeed as an organization it will be down to the dynamics of The Mirror Principle. Ensure to use The Mirror Principle for your success. With it there are Mirror Cleaners and Mirror Blurrers; forces which we have discussed on earlier pages. Both forces should be mastered. One of the areas we discussed was rest. Impatience was identified as a potential Mirror Blurrer and one of the ways to control impatience is to take rests. There will be times within your group where certain members need rest. In fact you should strive to have planned timeouts. These planned breaks give your members time to engage in other activities that they are interested in. This practice brings out the best in them because they come back recharged; it leaves them refreshed to continue the task at hand.

Great organizations create a balanced environment for their employees. Hence they increase productivity. Many observers have praised the Google model, and it serves the company's purpose. Google encourages employees to work around long term deadlines but at their own pace. Employees are treated to first class dining, gyms, laundry rooms, car washes, haircuts, massages, community buses, yoga classes and more; all within the workplace. This might not work for another business model such as a space agency but the underlying principle applies to all groups. It ensures that the lives of your employees are balanced, and the workplace is a place that they are happy to come to.

Nutshell

Organizations are set up for various reasons but every organization has a goal. Groups of persons come together to achieve a common purpose. However it is not only the presence of people that makes the group effective. Success as an organization starts with having the right blend of people. It is bolstered by giving these persons a vision to run with. When motivation is added to this, and everyone on the team is singing from the same hymnbook, success is not very far away.

A great organization recruits a team of dedicated researchers who increase the product's usefulness; skilful deliverers who build the product; passionate marketers who give the product relevance; and wise managers who provide direction to the other three.

The task of managers is made easier when the organization has a clear-cut image of what it stands for. The mirror brings this image to life. The mirror ushers in unity and fires up passion amongst the members of an organization. Then again every organization has a mirror. It is having the right mirror that matters. An organization without a clear image on its mind opens itself up to division; the multiplicity of visions. As old wisdom dictates, "a house that is divided against its own self shall not stand".

The great organizations encourage their members to look into the mirror. They do not just have a mirror; they reproduce it in the minds of members. The mirror image becomes the mental image they see as a group. Rather than look over their shoulders to occupy themselves with comparisons with their rivals, they look inward. They believe in their abilities and they set goals that make the best of their own potential. These ones have understood that there is room for everyone at the top. The successes of their rivals is only an opportunity to learn and be inspired; not an indication of their own failure. There has never been a time in human history when there was not enough room at the top. Opportunity will only cease to exist when all imagination is flushed out from the earth.

The union of minds creates what observers have called the fifth element. Up in the same bracket as earth, wind, fire and water is the Spirit of The Mob. It symbolizes the coming together of human minds fuelled by a high degree of passion. Together, these minds create an energy that can control a vast number of people. Unified thought in an organization is the wheel that drives the group in the direction of its goal.

8 The Mirror Principle And A Nation

The year was 1777. An army of twelve thousand brave soldiers camped at Valley Forge, Pennsylvania. Drawn from fourteen colonies, these soldiers stood watch to protect the land of their birth from further invasion by foreign masters. Poorly armed, and with very little military experience, the Americans passionately resisted the British rule; a rule they felt was not in their best interest. Their resistance in New York had failed. Squared up against the might of the most revered military force at the time, these courageous fighters had taken a massive beating. Led by George Washington they retreated; but only as far as Valley Forge. Where others would have retreated completely, these brave men and women defied the odds to defend their "new nation" as many called it. The might of Britain was not their only worry; the gory fangs of a cold and bitter winter was upon them.

Many among these soldiers had no shoes; the clothes they had on were barely sufficient. They were weary from battle and yet had to deal with disease, bad wounds and months of little food. They sheltered in tents that did little to ward off the harsh lashes of the cold winds. With few blankets and tattered garments, many of the soldiers died in that valley. Some reports say the deaths were over two thousand five hundred. Irregular food supplies meant they sometimes fed on a mixture of flour and water. Even the horses died of starvation. The hope of birthing a new nation was now turning into misery and despair. Against these odds, the soldiers kept faith. They longed for a coming dawn; a day when their land would be free from foreign rule and their people could choose their own fate. It is from the midst of these men that the following words, penned to paper by Thomas Paine, were written. Till this day these words reverberate through the heart of many human endeavours.

> *"These are times that try men's souls. The summer soldier and the sunshine patriot will, in this crisis, shrink from the service of their country; but he that stands by it now, deserves the love and thanks of man and woman. Tyranny, like hell, is not easily conquered; yet we have this consolation with us, that the harder the conflict, the more glorious the triumph. What we obtain*

The Mirror Principle

too cheap, we esteem too lightly: it is dearness only that gives everything its value."

Thomas Paine

The long winter of desolation turned into a spring of hope as these brave soldiers went on to conquer the mighty British army; they secured America's independence. They fought for one goal: to be free from foreign rule and forge a nation for themselves, of themselves, and by themselves. Their vision was to establish a nation where freedom was recognized and bravery was rewarded. At the very core of this passionate ideal the founding fathers of America created a document that they called The Declaration of American Independence. Today the United States of America is arguably the most successful nation on earth.

Unknown to some of those brave soldiers at Valley Forge, the pains they endured through those gruesome months of 1777 were labour pains that heralded the birth of a great nation. They believed in an ideal; they fought for that ideal. Today the ideal still forms the core on which they have succeeded as a nation. The first few lines of that ideal reads thus: "We hold these truths to be self-evident; that all men were created equal, and they have been endowed by their creator with certain unalienable rights and among these are life, liberty and the pursuit of happiness". The great nation of America was built on these words.

A wake-up call: Our National Duty

No matter what part of the world we hail from, we all belong to a nation. Fate has planted us in certain geographical locations. Through the actions of our forefathers we have found ourselves counted as part of one nation. Nobody exists without being a national of a certain country. It is true that the world is becoming one global village, but the dynamics of world economy constantly remind us that we are citizens of a particular country.

Our citizenship to a nation entitles us, or should entitle us, to have a voice on anything that affects the nation; from how her resources are used to what direction the nation should go. Our standard of living is to a large extent tied to the fate of our nation. Some nations are well advanced in their provision of comfortable standards of living to their citizens in comparison to others. Hence the world is inundated with labels like first world and third world, developed and developing countries, established and emerging markets, industrialized and non-industrialized among others. Whichever category your nation finds itself in, it is a product of The Mirror Principle. In a sense you cannot change your nation of birth. Just like you cannot choose your family, your nation is a natural endowment from birth. Helping the nation chart its course is a duty that you share with fellow citizens of the nation. Your nation is as much your property as it is the property of the prime minister, president, or any other leader.

Pause For A Moment; Realize Who You Are

We all do ourselves a huge favour when we take time out to reflect on who we are and where we are living today. The pressures of daily life could fill our minds so much that we fail to appreciate our existence in the grand scheme of things. Somehow it is easy to forget that we are only one generation in a very long line of human history. Our minds are ever so bogged down by the worries of how to survive in life. We fail to ponder on the things that really matter. The big questions like "How did we get here?" "What makes everyone different?" "What goes on inside our bodies?" "What is happening to the other species around us?" "How and where did my great great grandfather live?" There are thousands of other questions that carry as much significance as "What do I wear?" "What do I eat?" "How much money can I make?" "How do I pay off my mortgage?" We need to pause sometimes, and reflect on the big questions. Too many of us live life as though it were a rat race; a daily burden that we must carry; a struggle for survival. I call this The Closet Mentality. We need to get out of the Closet Mentality as often as we can.

We often forget that the world is a place of vast features. The world goes beyond our small worlds that we live in. It helps to remind ourselves that earth, our mighty planet, is only one of millions of bodies in space. There are startling discoveries that suggest that the future may hold evidence of life on another planet. Now back to our planet; we know there are over seven billion people living around us. If we were to count all the people that dwell on earth with us, it would take close to three lifetimes to count everyone even if we were counting as fast as one person per second. That is how many we are. Science can date human existence to as far back as a hundred and sixty thousand years. Going by this alone, our generation could be labelled as the five thousandth generation of humans to live on earth. This figure is not a proven fact; if anything we might be much more advanced than five thousand. So the point is that we are just one of thousands of generations that have lived on earth. Like the generations past, we would paint our part of the big picture of human history. Then when our time here comes to a conclusion, we will inevitably lay down the paintbrushes for the coming generation to continue from where we stopped.

Has it ever crossed your mind that right there where you are standing, or over at the park where you relax there is a chance that human beings from a generation of a thousand years back inhabited the same place. It is a priceless feeling when we connect with history. To reason in this way helps you to appreciate the fact that we are a unique part of a very long chain called the human race.

Mankind has always lived in communities, or what we could call nations. Over the periods of human history, some nations have risen by force, fortuity, or craft to dominate and lead others. This domination usually symbolises a new era, but the period of domination by a certain nation usually comes to an end after some time. Hence we have had different dispensations; each with a leading light amongst the nations; each with a recognizable dominant force. As the saying goes, 'for every ten kings there are ten epochs'.

The Great Civilizations and The Mirror Principle

Five thousand years ago, long before most of the things we know ever existed, the balance of power rested in North

Africa. Along the Nile River, in present day Egypt, there existed a highly resourceful group of people. They established a powerful system that would go down in history as the Egyptian Civilization. The Egyptians employed The Mirror Principle to attain their status as a superpower, but they may not have been aware of it. The first thing these wise people did was to assess the resources they had within their borders. They looked among their people and across their land to gain knowledge of their potential. Rather than wage aimless wars against their neighbours, the Egyptians studied their abilities and devised ways of turning their natural wealth into national prosperity.

All they had at the time was the Nile River; but this was enough. They adapted their farming seasons to the conditions of the Nile River valley. The Egyptians created a sophisticated irrigation system, which ensured that the fertile valley produced abundant crops. This spurred the nation into becoming a strong trading force; its economy soared beyond measure. Soon, with its ever-increasing wealth, Egypt wisely invested in other areas of its national life. It established a strong educational system; vigorously harnessed its vast mineral resources; enhanced communication amongst its people by developing a unique writing system, and promoted the use of arts and literature. Ruled by a Pharaoh and held together by common religious beliefs the Egyptians also assembled a strong military force. As its economic might grew so did its political dominance. The Egyptian empire soon stretched into Syria and present day Palestine.

Egypt's success as a superpower ensured that her era in human civilization is forever etched on the walls of history. Some of the remarkable inventions which the Egyptians gifted to all of humanity include monuments like obelisks, temples, pyramids, the first known ships, the science of medicine, glass technology, new forms of literature, sophisticated agricultural techniques, the basic tenets of mathematics, and many others.

Just when the Egyptian empire was reaching a crescendo, humans in another part of the world were building their great nation as well. After two thousand years of Egyptian prominence the compass of history moved from North Africa to the Italian Peninsula. Roughly eight hundred years before the landmark event of the birth of Jesus Christ, the Roman civilization was born. The Roman nation was built on one vision: to dominate the entire Mediterranean axis through superior military force. From a group predominantly made up of livestock farmers, the Romans used The Mirror Principle to build a powerful nation; arguably the greatest empire in recorded history.

KJB

***

The Roman nation established itself on a system of government where every citizen had a voice. Leaders from amongst the people were voted into power to represent the people's interest. The Romans then invested in their military prowess; backed by a people in search of global dominance. Led by clever generals like Julius Caesar and Pompey, they soon overcame the aggression of their neighbours Gaul. Over a few hundred years the Romans had conquered many surrounding kingdoms, and became the dominant people of the Mediterranean area. They followed this up with the conquests of Hispania, North Africa, and other overseas nations. The Romans had established themselves as the most successful imperial power.

In accomplishing their goal of political dominance, the Romans wisely invested in not only their agricultural resources but in their people. The nation spent vast resources on technology, educating its people, and promoting arts and literature. Some of the icons that helped create the Roman success story were Caesar, Cicero, Pompey and Horace.

The national successes of Rome and Egypt are noteworthy. However there have existed some other remarkable nations in history whose impact on humankind cannot be overemphasized. These nations not only achieved success, but they gave humankind many reasons to believe that almost anything is possible when men come together with a common purpose. Two of such nations were the Mayans and the Chinese.

***

The Mayans were settled in the Americas just over 30 generations ago. The Mayan people experienced a surge in intellectual pursuits during that period. This surge was the result of a collective commitment of the Mayan people to champion the cause of scientific discovery. They unveiled some amazing findings and innovations to the world. They developed a groundbreaking concept of written language, built the stepped pyramids, reported some extremely accurate astronomical observations, introduced the concept of zero in the field of mathematics, and developed the Mayan numerals and the famous Mayan calendar.

***

The Chinese civilization of 200 BC was a golden age in Chinese history. Spanning over several centuries and controlling over 40 million people, the Chinese empowered their people with strong leadership and education. Science and technology made notable advances and economic prosperity followed. The Chinese era introduced the concept of negative numbers in mathematics, the act of papermaking, navigation instruments amongst many other things. This nation also built a sophisticated wall of defence that made its borders impenetrable for many years. The Great Chinese wall still remains a masterpiece; a testament to human industry; a tribute to the power of collective purpose.

***

We also recall the Greek era; a civilization that spanned several centuries. The Greek nation blazed the trail for many economic, scientific, and literary achievements still celebrated till this day. In this nation, knowledge was regarded as the key to economic and political dominance. The Greeks set the pace for human advancements in philosophy, literature, mathematics, architecture, science, and technology. By the 4th and 5th centuries BC, Greece was the world's most developed economy. Inspired by icons like Alexander the Great, Aristotle, Plato, and Pythagoras, the Greeks represented a beacon of light in an age plagued by periods of darkness.

***

More recently we have witnessed two other great civilizations; and there is the promise of more to come. We have had the great industrial revolution led by the British nation just over two hundred and fifty years ago. During this period the Great British Empire established an enormous economic structure around the world; it opened the gates for thousands of astonishing inventions. The economic benefits of inventions like the telephone, electric power generation, railways, aircrafts, steel, and many others have piloted humankind to yet another level.

Today we recognize yet another superpower in the United States of America. From a collection of scattered colonies to becoming the most powerful nation on the planet within a space of two centuries is a truly remarkable feat. America is a nation built on the infallible foundations of collective purpose.

America, Britain, Ancient Greece, Rome, and China have all shown that if any nation would invest in its collective potential, and stay true to a common ideal, their success is only a short distance away. On the flip side, some of these civilizations have also shown us that no matter how successful you are as a nation, you could get on the wrong side of The Mirror Principle, and plummet to your ruin. For success to be maintained, the same principles that brought you success have to be embraced without ending. A simple departure from the recipe that brought national success could bring a giant to its knees. Success would not return until all that went wrong had been made right.

We are now going to take a look at how the three components of The Mirror Principle could be identified in a nation. Perhaps when we understand this we could take another look at our nation and get it on the right track to success. The goal of our nation may not be to become a superpower. However, the fulfilment of its citizens is a basic obligation owed to every citizen. The Mirror Principle could be leveraged to help a nation achieve its own greatness. For those already great nations, they can look to The Mirror Principle to understand how it lifted them to their present status, and how they can best sustain their greatness. We shall study some examples of nations that succeeded using The Mirror Principle, and nations that failed because of The Mirror Principle. Indeed every civilization, dispensation, or national era rises and falls on The Mirror Principle.

"Your Perception of Your Potential is Your Reality"
The Mirror Principle

The potential implies the seed of the nation; perception implies the vision of the nation. Vision in this context goes beyond a mere dream. It points to the focus and collective mentality of a nation. Perception is the mind of the nation. The product of mind and seed is reality. No nation is justified to blame another entirely for its misfortunes just as a bird with wings cannot blame other birds for its inability to fly.

The Seed of A Nation

All nations are blessed with a seed. Every nation has potential; raw gifts waiting to be harnessed and shared with the world. The seed of a nation is its ticket to everything that it dreams of becoming. In this realization lies an inevitable truth: Every nation is blessed with inherent greatness. Some nations have realized this; some have started to realize it while many more are yet to scratch the surface of their potential. Perhaps one of the most appalling facts of human existence is the stark presence of abject poverty in many parts of the world. Among these same poor countries are some of the most endowed nations on earth. The citizens of these nations live in misery while they sit on top of vast wealth. Around the world today we see typical cases that portray the ecclesiastical text of "princes walking as slaves on the earth".

The seed of a nation speaks of its potential. A nation's potential comprises its raw abilities, its skills, its powers, its resources, and literally anything that it has that could make it a great nation. So how do you know a nation's potentials? If you take a close look you would find that there are three facets to a nation's seed. Each one must be properly harnessed to yield the fruits of greatness and national prosperity. These three facets are: its natural resources, its history, and its human capital.

Natural Resources

Everything that exists on earth is either a natural resource, or is composed of natural resources at its most basic level. Natural resources are almost as diverse as human beings. From the ubiquitous resources like water and sunlight, to localized resources like oil, rubber, metal ores, forests, animals, and gas, every nation is blessed with substantial resources. The fact that some of these resources have not been discovered does not mean that they do not exist. The nation of Nigeria for instance did not realize it was sitting on vast amounts of oil, otherwise known as the black gold, until just over forty years ago. The discovery of this natural resource quickly catapulted the nation into worldly significance. Russia is lavished with vast reserves of natural gas. Over the last century, as the technology for piping gas has become more advanced, the economic power of Russia has soared.

The Mirror Principle

Natural resources are there to be discovered, researched, enjoyed, and replenished. Any nation that would invest in the study, use, and reproduction of its natural resources is on its way to economic prosperity. Norway is one of the smallest countries in the world, but it is the third largest oil producer in the world. It accounts for a third of all the gas supplies in the European Union although it occupies less than one percent of the landmass of Europe. Just over fifty years ago Norway invested heavily into researching its potentials. It studied the natural resources that existed within its borders. Soon it discovered oil and natural gas in huge quantities, and it invested in the extraction of oil and gas; resources that could remain the mainstay of the world's energy sector for at least another five decades. Through the use of this potential, Norway has moved up from a struggling nation in the 1940s to a nation with the highest human development index ranking in the world. In another mark of brilliance, Norway has invested the returns from this wealth not only in its citizen's welfare, but also in harnessing other natural resources to sustain its economic stability. This is the mark of a nation that has successfully lifted itself on the back of its own potentials.

Lazy nations tend to blame the prosperity of other nations for their own misery or poverty. In today's world where statistical evidence and technological advancements paint undeniable pictures of what we truly are, the blame-it-on-the-others excuse does not hold water. On earlier pages we talked about the dangers of the scarcity mentality. Some nations have fallen into the quagmire of thinking that their natural resources are either too few or not good enough. Such nations do not invest in their natural resources because they believe these resources are not good enough for the world stage. This erroneous belief is the source of their poverty; the circle of their insanity; indeed their miserable fate. Where other nations see potential, these lazy nations look only to their lack and the negative sides of their potential.

Potential never appears as amazing as its end results. The seed is never as glorious as the garden it produces. Carbon in its initial state appears to have little value until its potential is harnessed into amazing diamonds. For this reason a nation commits economic suicide anytime it disregards the natural resources that she has been gifted with. Until two and a half centuries ago an enormous potential lay in the rubber trees of South America, but it was yet undiscovered. In 1735 an inquisitive geographer took samples of this tree and started a decade of research that revealed tremendous opportunities. Soon the reigning superpower at the time, the English, caught wind of its usefulness and planted the seeds around most of its colonies. The rubber tree was also discovered in nations like

Liberia and Nigeria but it was the British Malaya (now Malaysia) and their neighbours in Asia that cultivated this natural resource with tact and vigour. Today three countries namely Thailand, Indonesia and Malaysia together account for over seventy percent of global natural rubber production. Ironically the continent of South America where rubber was first discovered is not regarded as a big player in this commodity on the world stage. The relevance of rubber to today's world is obvious. If you take a look around your present surroundings chances are that you would see many things produced from this resource.

Natural resources sometimes lie in hidden reserves and require intense research and effort to extract them. Examples of these hidden gems are oil, gold, uranium, and other precious metals. A nation that is willing to prosper should not renege from the daunting tasks that research and extraction entail. The tasks are even more daunting because these stages are fraught with showstoppers and disappointments. However, it is a testament to a nation's determination when it remains true to harnessing its potentials; not just those that are readily available, but the natural resources that lie deep within its shores.

Not all natural resources are hidden from apparent view. Indeed some of a nation's valuable resources are visible and abundant. The United States of America could have easily relegated the relevance of corn. It could have labelled corn as a grain fit only for domestic consumption. It could have concluded that the corn plant has a tendency to grow under any climate so cultivating vast amounts of it would yield little value. Such is the tenacity of the American nation that they ignored these logical theories and invested heavily into corn research. The results of this acknowledgement of potential speak for itself. The United States produces almost half of the corn output in today's world. The corn grain has since been discovered as a huge source of ethanol, medicine ingredients, edible oil, sweeteners, beverages and livestock feed. Experts have found over four thousand uses for corn; majority of them have a favourable impact on the environment. Corn now accounts for close to ten percent of the United States agricultural exports.

In the story we told about the Egyptian civilization we see another vital use of natural resources. In this case the natural resource was as readily available as sunlight. The great Egyptian civilization sprung up from the discovery of a good use for water. The ancient Egyptians lived along the River Nile in North Eastern Africa. After witnessing the richness of the soil within the delta area, the Egyptians constructed sophisticated irrigation systems that spread the flow of water beyond its previous limits. This way they turned their nation from an infertile desert into an agricultural stronghold.

History

Many nations realise the importance of their natural resources, but only a few recognise the second vital aspect of their national potential: Their history. Every nation has a history. A nation's history is simply a story of the past events and persons that are directly connected to that nation.

A nation that is unaware of its history is like a person who has lost his memory. It is never a perfect story; neither is it always one to be entirely proud of. Yet a nation's history is its best teacher. When history is properly recorded, like a visit to the cinemas, we can sit back and watch events as they played out. Our history is a looking glass that shows us our successes and our failures. With this great armoury at our disposal we can recognize ourselves. Through our history we can learn about the things we are capable of. We also discover the pitfalls to avoid; the decisions that made or marred us; the attributes that elevated or weakened us. History mirrors our strengths and weaknesses.

There is hardly anything that binds a nation more than its history. Immense motivation could come from the past events that the nation has experienced. Somehow both the good and bad experiences forge a nation's identity. Whenever a nation is brought up in the minds of its citizens they tend to recall the people and events that best describe their history. This they do by the principle of association that we have talked about earlier in this book. It is for this reason that certain national icons spring into mind at the mention of some nations. India has Mahatma Gandhi, England has Her Majesty the Queen, and South Africa has Nelson Mandela. These persons symbolize the rich history of their respective nations. They are the rallying point of national passion; the hallmarks of patriotism.

If passion is vital to any fulfilling endeavour then history is essential to a nation. A nation's passion and the patriotism of its citizens are inextricably tied to her experiences. No matter how dark or traumatic those experiences were, they form the core reason why a nation would come together and strive towards a common goal. These experiences do not merely refer to individuals like Gandhi or Mandela but in many cases, they are a culmination of significant events that took place within the nation. You only need to look at the face of an American trooper when the national anthem, The Star Spangled Banner, is being sung to witness a strong passion for country. On that one face we clearly see a proud reflection into the country's past, a sudden acknowledgement of her past struggles, and a resolve to ensure that the labours of the forefathers is never in vain; at least not in their lifetime. The Russians, Chinese, Germans and the British display an undeniable patriotism forged under the heat of their brightest experiences; hardened in the aftermath of their darkest hours. A patriotic nation is one that is aware of its history.

What is about to be said may not be scientifically verifiable, but it is difficult to shove aside the impact of lives that were lost for the sake of a cause. When blood is shed for a cause; when the sacred lives of human beings are taken from them as they fight for a cause or defend a nation; a stream of energy is being released into the history of that nation or cause. For this reason the death of Jesus Christ forms the central motivating factor in the realm of Christianity. America will remember the founding fathers who risked their lives to win an almost impossible freedom. She would also remember the brave firefighters of September 11th, 2001 who gave their lives on the call of duty to their nation. It is almost as if their blood waters the seeds of the nation's future greatness.

You can hardly visit Scotland and not sense their history as a nation; a wave of reminiscence hits you as you walk its streets. There are monuments and landmarks that depict the travails of her freedom fighters; amongst them are Robert the Bruce and William Wallace. In the case of William Wallace, faced between the choice of obtaining mercy if he denies the sovereignty of Scotland and a horrific death, he chose to die for his country. Through his martyrdom Scotland the dream became Scotland the reality. History has it that William Wallace was dragged by a horse throughout the city. He was hanged, castrated, and had his bowels burnt before his own eyes before he was beheaded. His courage spurred the Scots to many victories, and till this day the patriotism of the Scotsman is still fuelled by the energy released from one man's fatal act of courage.

Human Capital

The collective potential of its citizens is arguably the most important facet of the seed of a nation. A nation is only as great as the sum of the giftedness of its citizens. Unlike an organization a nation cannot recruit all of her citizens. A nation's citizens are determined by fate; not by a planned recruitment process.

In this light a nation's task is to develop the individual capabilities of each of its citizens. It must understand that all human beings are endowed with a gift. As such each citizen has something to offer; a role to play in the nation's greatness. Every nation has its share of thinkers, science lovers, sportsmen, military men, architects and farmers. The difference between a highly developed and underdeveloped nation is the value they place on their citizens. A great nation sees its citizens as one more contributor to its overall success. In stark contrast, a miserable nation views a citizen as one more consumer of its scarce resources.

To build a great nation the skillsets of its people must be developed. A nation in pursuit of growth must present its citizens with an environment that encourages their abilities. As a whole is the sum of the parts, each citizen must be catered for. When a citizen is well looked after, that citizen soon becomes an asset to the nation. Her natural skills become evident and her exploits contribute to the success of the nation.

Great nations do not only keep their citizens; they improve their human capital by encouraging skilled people from other countries to join their fold. In doing so, they increase their potential to succeed. One of the reasons for the success of the United Kingdom is its strategic encouragement of obvious talent from other nations to work for its purpose. By creating a conducive environment for skills to thrive and by rewarding such talents, the United Kingdom has established itself at the summit of world power. A visit to the capital city of London drives this point home. You will observe a collection of diverse people with great depth and remarkable qualities. Little wonder why the city is the financial hub of the world.

Japan is a prime example of a nation that has risen from the ashes of underdevelopment to the pinnacle of world power. About a hundred years ago, Japan freed itself from the stranglehold of tradition and destructive cultural dogmas. It embraced a sophisticated education system where all people regardless of age, class and gender were encouraged to attend schools up to university level. Vocational studies were also encouraged. Japan's economic growth went on a downward spiral during the Second World War. In this period it suffered the atomic bombing of Hiroshima and Nagasaki; one of the most debilitating annihilations in the history of military warfare.

The Japanese spirit was not to be exterminated. Although many lives, buildings and enterprises were destroyed by a brutal war, the resolve of the Japanese nation was intact. If anything, it grew even stronger. Japan went back to the same approach that made it Asia's superpower. It rebuilt its human capital. Education was made mandatory for all its citizens. She retained her skilled citizens and attracted skilled foreigners to work for her interests. Within twenty years of the devastating war Japan rose to the summit of world economic power. This economic growth would become known as the Japan Post-War Economic Miracle. Her human capital development has surpassed that of the United Kingdom and United States on many occasions with a corresponding economic growth rate. Today Japan remains one of the largest economies in the world. She is home to many great symbols of human enterprise like Toyota, Sony, Honda, the Tokyo Stock Exchange, and Nintendo. It surprises nobody therefore that she has one of the lowest unemployment rates in the world. Japan has produced as many as fifteen Nobel Laureates in the fields of physics, medicine and chemistry. Over fifteen percent of Forbes Global 2000 companies started out in Japan.

The obvious point here is that human capital is vital to every nation. You may have all the resources in the world, but you need the right skillsets to turn these resources into national prosperity.

Every nation should recognise, respect, and nurture its seed. Her natural resources, history, and human capital all constitute her potential.

The Mirror Of A Nation

There are many wonders in the world as we know it. There are some wonders that exist whose reasons for existence are not easily explained. One of such wonders is national image. It seems as though everyone in the world agrees on their national image. Take five people from the same country, and the chances are that each person would relate to you the exact same image that they hold about their country. Take another five people from another country, and their image of their nation is likely to be identical. Folks could differ on their perception of a brand or individual but people rarely disagree on the image they hold about their nation. I am not able to ascribe an explanation to this, but it goes to show that national image is as straightforward as it is potent.

Every nation has an image, and hence a mirror. In a nation's life, constantly held before it, is a mirror that impresses an image of itself on the nation. The mirror determines how the nation views itself, and how others view her. The mirror controls the mindset of the nation. The citizens of the nation see a reflection in the mirror, and they act according to what they see. The mirror of a nation tells a nation, "This is who you are" and "This is what you are going to become". Unless that image is changed in the collective mentality of its citizens, a nation is resigned to becoming the image in the mirror. Mirrors are that powerful. They form the basis of self-image, which in turn controls our actions, perceptions, and our fate.

The positive side to the presence of the mirror in our national lives is that the mirror is a function of our own design. We can create our own mirror. We may already have a national mirror, but we can tear that apart, and uphold a new mirror. Mirrors are not agents of predestination; they are tools for achievement. A nation is not doomed by the present image it sees on its mirror. A nation is doomed by its unwillingness to take down that mirror, and put up a mirror that reflects its greatness.

"Your Perception of Your Potential is Your Reality"
The Mirror Principle

Some nations have an image of a land of freedom, bravery and prosperity. Some nations see themselves as the cultural heartbeat of the world. Some have a national image of being the cradle of technology and innovation. Some see themselves as the harbingers of peace and tranquillity. Sadly some nations see themselves as doomed by corruption and scarcity of resources. They paint a picture of hopelessness and despondency for themselves. As they do, they inadvertently steer their nation into the abyss of depravity and human denigration. A strong cycle is then created. What you see of yourself, you act as. The world sees your action, and label you based on those actions. So inadvertently, you are being labelled based on what you see about yourself.

Civilizations have risen and fallen on vision; the mirror image they held up for themselves. The Egyptians saw an empire thriving in agriculture and leading in scientific discoveries. They thrived on their intelligence and economic prowess. However as soon as the Nile River began to dry up, their image turned into lack and panic. Rather than rely on the same attitude of innovation that brought them success, they were blinded by the shortage on the Nile River. In a swift change of fortunes, the world's greatest nation was swept aside into obscurity.

The Greek nation ruled the world at some point in human history. They were revered for their human capital and their rare ability to turn less promising materials into exciting innovations. To an extent, Greeks saw themselves as demigods. For years, they dictated the advancements of the human race in the fields of astronomy, mathematics, art, philosophy, and military strategy. Aristotle, Socrates and Plato introduced many great things including the system of democracy to the world but failed to carry the vision to generations after them. When these great Greeks died, the image died with them.

When a nation decides to hold up conflicting mirror images of itself, division which means a multiplicity of visions occurs. Division breeds disunity; a recipe for destruction. Many of the failed civilizations once had a unified vision. Over time they became weakened because citizens could not agree on a common image for themselves. Rome gave the world the most powerful empire in recorded history. It led the world through a strong vision of military power. In a fatal bid to satisfy diverse egos, the empire was split into western and eastern governments. Rome had grown so big that the Roman ideology that had won her so many victories was now lost on many of its people. Corruption became the order of the day. Soon Rome lost most of its power and dominance. This underlines the importance of a single vision for a nation.

Sages Elixir

"The multitude that is not brought to act as a unity is confusion. That unity which has not its origin in the multitude is tyranny."

Pascal Blaise

National Ideology Is The Mirror

To put this in simple terms, the mirror of a nation is its national ideology. An ideology is central to a nation's growth. It is the image of itself; the idea that it represents. It is no coincidence that the underdeveloped nations of the world lack a clear national ideology. Conversely the developed nations demonstrate a clear ideology. The founding fathers of the United States of America lifted up a mirror in 1776. This mirror was and still is the national image impressed on the minds of the citizens of the nation. When William Jefferson, John Adams, Benjamin Franklin and fifty-three others penned down and signed the Declaration of Independence, that mirror was created. It proposed the vision for America; an ideology for her people. America envisioned a land of the free; a home to the brave.

For the last two hundred years, every so often, the people of America look into this mirror to remind themselves of who they are. Each time the nation's resolve is tested its citizens look to this mirror, and it gives them strength and direction. Again by the powerful principle of transference of energy a nation's citizens are empowered with hope, strength, and belief that resonate out of the mirror. We remember not so long ago, when the evil monster of racial prejudice sought to divide the American nation. If there was anything that formed the rallying point to save the nation from the brink of civil disaster, it was the great mirror of the United States of America. As citizens of all roots and races looked up at the same mirror created by the founding fathers it opened their eyes to who they truly were; a land of promise where in the words of Martin Luther

King Jr. "people live in a nation where they would not be judged by the colour of their skin but rather by the content of their character". The most profound effect of a national mirror is that it stands as the ultimate judge in the times of crisis, and crisis is inevitable; the rallying point in the days when citizens disagree on what direction to take.

When a nation holds a clear ideology its codes of conduct, constitution, short and long term goals all fall in line with that ideology. It is like the backbone for all the actions taken by a nation; the ultimate dream upon which the nation finds its fulfilment. When a nation lacks an ideology, they lack vision. A nation without an ideology is like a blind horse; galloping to nowhere; headed for catastrophe.

The mirror as we know it has two sides to it. The first is the image of who you are at present. The second is who you could become. Any nation that wishes to progress may not be able to alter who they have become as they are unable to change their past. The great power they possess is creating the right image for the future. When we talked about citizens agreeing on the image of their nation we were referring to their perception of their history. However the more relevant agreement that citizens need to achieve is the image of what they could become. A nation's mirror is its ideology. It says, "this is what we want to be" and, "this is what we shall become". In holding that mirror right in front of their eyes they put themselves in the prime position to become the image in the mirror. Even the universe would seem to aid them to achieve their national greatness.

It is comforting to know that there is not only one national ideology that guarantees success. The truth is that any national ideology that means well for her citizens and is built around the seed of the nation, shall bestow greatness on the nation. China may not see itself as the land of the free but it sees itself as a model for economic, sustainable and scientific development.

At every point in this book where we have mentioned mirrors, we have always mentioned the concept of reinforcers in about the same breath. Reinforcers multiply the appearance of the vision; they amplify the message of the mirror. The minds of a nation's citizenry are a battlefield. There is a constant war between the national ideology and other ideas from external forces. Hence a nation should be vigilant in placing strategic reminders in the minds of its citizens about what they stand for and where they are headed. We have discovered on the pages of this book that sensory perception is the doorway to the mind. It is important to flood the sensory perception of citizens with the nation's vision, and what they represent to the world. The national ideology is not supposed to be written on parched papers alone, or stored in national archives; it should be written and stored in the minds of its citizens.

To achieve this level of enlightenment for all its citizens, a nation should make use of tools that reinforce the national vision. For this reason, every nation has a flag, an emblem, and an anthem. These reinforcers are a constant reminder to her citizens about the nation's core values. There are many in this world whose emotions are stirred when they hear their national anthem. For some it is the flag that reminds them of the essence of their nation. For others it is events performed by the nation's heroes or other citizens; events that remind them of the vision of the nation; events that awaken them to their duty to their nation.

Adolf Hitler is certainly not the most loved figure in human history, but it is staggering to know that he used The Mirror Principle to great effect. He understood the power of reinforcers in enforcing a nation's ideology. He understood the fickle nature of the human mind. He knew that if he said the same things over and over again to the same people, and if they listened, no matter how untrue his assertions were, they would soon begin to believe him. He wrote and sold the Mein Kampf to the German nation. In a short space of time he had successfully permeated an entire nation with Nazi ideology.

How did he do this? It was through the use of reinforcers. Hitler used social media, symbols, artworks, books, pamphlets, and posters to flood the sensory perception of the citizenry. He won their eyes and ears, and consequently won their hearts and minds. One man convinced an entire nation of well-meaning people that the Aryan race was more superior to any other race in the world. He flooded German minds with information that was sometimes untrue, but strong enough to whip up sentiments in the hearts of the citizens of the nation. Hitler once admitted to his generals that "I will provide propaganda; its credibility does not matter. The victor will never be asked if his words were true". Asides Hitler, history is replete with stories of nations whose image of themselves have been forged by leaders or founders who understood the power of using reinforcers to establish the national vision.

As a nation's citizens hold on to one national image, this image drives their actions and short-term goals. Successful nations always have a step-by-step plan on how to achieve their ultimate goal. They formulate short and long-term project plans. They set targets that they can reach. All of these plans and targets are all driven by the ultimate national dream. When the national ideology is clear, people tend to understand the short-term goals better, and strive towards national achievement.

The Mind Of A Nation

Every nation has a soul; a collective mentality that inexplicably captures the moods and the beliefs of that nation. There is an energy that flows within a nation that is sometimes almost tangible. This is why frequent travellers tend to talk about the peculiar feel of a place. It is almost as though a place has a personality. Sometimes you sense this national psyche when in the presence of a group of people from the same nation. They collectively tend to send out a certain vibe that you feel, but may not be able to describe in words. This feeling is a pointer to a profound truth: Every nation has a soul; her own mind.

The mind is the seat of emotions, knowledge and beliefs. These key forms of energy impact all our actions; both conscious and unconscious actions. At every point in time, a nation is sending out signals from its mind. It draws on the dominant thoughts of its citizens and takes the shape of these thoughts. When the people of a nation think of criminal thoughts, the mind of the nation is one of corruption. If the people think noble thoughts the mind of the nation is pure and noble. If the people are passionate about a positive vision you could almost feel the positive energy once you arrive at the country's borders or engage her citizens. When the people are filled with thoughts of hate and scepticism the negative energy strikes you in much the same way.

This trend becomes important in the context of war and its detrimental effects. A civil war is an exhibition of a conflict of minds. When a nation is caught in two or more minds it suffers from the chaos that is bound to ensue. Peace and stability are the hallmarks of a great nation. This is only achieved when the people are of one mind. We talked about the success of Norway earlier in terms of the value they place on their natural resources. It is also important to note that Norway matches her talent with a high degree of responsibility and stability. In fact while other oil rich countries levy as low as thirty percent tax on major oil multinationals, Norway imposes as much as ninety percent tax on these same firms. Do these multinationals shy away from Norway's energy wealth? The answer is no. All the major oil firms are operating in Norway. There is one simple reason for this: Norway is a nation of stability and transparency. A nation aspiring to achieve and sustain greatness should first pursue peace and stability; this requires oneness of mind.

We often see the soul of a nation come alive through her culture. Although culture is mostly inherited, the soul of a nation gives it life. Culture is a way of life; it shows the values that the nation holds dear. When a nation's cultural values promote respect for her senior citizens, support for children, acknowledgment of the sanctity of human life, and reward for good or honest labour, that nation is likely to achieve her fulfilment.

Some people remark that it is impossible to have all the citizens of a nation thinking the same thoughts at all times. This observation is correct. However we should remember that The Mirror Principle does not operate on all of our thoughts. The Mirror Principle thrives on dominant thought. Dominant thought is the thought that is associated with the highest belief or deepest emotion in the mind. A nation's dominant thought is the dominant thought of her citizens. If a nation has a vision and majority of her people focus their energies on seeing that vision to fruition, this is the prime example of dominant thought in action. To achieve a national vision, the people that drive the nation should have a collective mentality for success that dominates all other conflicting thoughts.

This brings up an interesting angle to national success. The question that arises is "Does every single citizen need to buy into a national ideology or vision for that nation to succeed?" We shall allow the history of great nations, both past and present, to provide the answer. Extensive studies by historians and sociologists show that all national ideologies are birthed by a small group of minds; sometimes representing less than one millionth of the national population. What usually happens is that a small group of people whom we could call the core group create an ideology and sell it to a wider audience. This second bracket, the wider audience, is not the whole population. The wider audience usually comprises of the educated persons within the nation. That then leaves us with a third bracket; a massive group of people who are barely literate, or do not understand how the nation works. The more developed a nation is, the less people you would have in the third bracket. In most cases the people in the third bracket follow the lead of the educated class because they trust and depend on them.

This book does not promote stratification of society in any form; it only portrays the trend as it is today. It appears that every nation, when it comes to the creation of its soul, could be broken down into three distinct brackets: The Directors who dictate the ideology; The Managers who support and promote the ideology; The Masses who trust the lead of the managers and tend to do what they are told to do. Most times this stratification is a direct result of education. The more education a citizen receives the more likely that citizen is going to move up the ladder across these three brackets.

The Mirror Principle

In today's world the bracket that individuals find themselves is entirely up to them. In fact many of the people who have risen to the group of directors started out among the masses. These persons applied themselves to education, and hence became a part of the engine that drives the nation. The directors set the mood and the managers promote that mood; the masses act out the mood.

To answer the pending question, the soul of a nation requires the collective support of a majority of its people. However the nation finds its essence in the minds of a core group; the leaders, the educated men and women who drive the nation. The directors and managers determine the direction of the nation, and they take the masses with them.

Sages Elixir

"Never doubt that a small group of thoughtful, committed citizens can change the world. Indeed, it is the only thing that ever has"

Margaret Mead

"No tyranny of circumstance can imprison a determined will for too long"

Orison S. Marden

Nutshell

The greatest changes in the history of the world have been started by a small group; not by whole nations; not by thousands; not even by hundreds. The great events that signalled turning points in human history have always begun with the thoughts of a small group of persons. In some cases, it started from a single person. A nation may quietly yearn for a certain dispensation, but it only takes one person or a small group of persons to bring these thoughts into life.

The great nations of today all seem to have embodied the same principles on their way to achieving greatness. It usually begins with a major challenge facing the nation. This challenge creates a stream of thought. A core group of persons believe in this thought and they promote this thought. Sooner or later, that which started off as a little spark spreads through the nation. Soon the majority of the people are in agreement to that thought. The nation begins to aspire towards a new cause; they see a new image. Soon the nation takes a new direction. This is The Mirror Principle at work.

Whether the direction brings the country to fulfilment is a totally different story. If we look at the nations that have been successful, they have achieved success by first understanding their potentials. They studied their citizens and recognized their abilities. They looked within themselves and discovered their national resources. They looked back at their past and honoured their history.

With potential understood, these nations proceeded to carving out an image for themselves. They closed their eyes to their present circumstances, and they created a vision of the nation they wanted to become. They understood the power of sensory perception, and they flooded the hearts of their citizens with this vision. Their national ideology became a rallying point.

As a final step, they got everyone working together. They promoted unity. They used the power of vision to forge oneness of mind. As we have stated on many occasions, it is impossible to contain a united force of people; who have potential and are persuaded about their potential.

The civilizations of old were all built on The Mirror Principle. Sadly, when these civilizations crumbled, they fell because of The Mirror Principle. To sustain national success a nation has to master the art of staying on the right side of The Mirror Principle.

9 The Mirror Principle and Children

Midnight was about an hour away. Nineteen year old Tania braved the biting cold and drizzles of snow as she posed by the roadside. It did not matter to her that it was Christmas Eve or that she was dressed too scantily for the harsh weather. In her line of work her body needed to be exposed; only dressed like Thanksgiving turkey; desperate to be priced. Her customers were fun seekers and drunkards; in fact anyone who could give her some money. Tonight, as she had done for the last three years, she would give herself to abuse, pain and torture. It was the only way she knew how to survive. Self-pity was a waste of time these days. She was a prostitute not because she enjoyed it; her brief life had taught her it was her only chance to continue to exist. The only other option was death.

To eat her next meal or pay the rent for a roof over her head she had to earn it with whatever she had left. With no education, no visible gifts, no family or friend, she felt that asking for a more comfortable life was asking for too much.

"Life is not fair and some are born to live in misfortune and poverty", she would say to herself every time she saw people her age having a good time.

Tania recalled today was now exactly three years since she first started out as a prostitute. An ex-boyfriend, now a pimp, had introduced her to the trade. She was desperately grateful to him. At last she had found something she could offer for which people were willing to hand her money. It was tortuous and debasing on most nights, but at least she was never hungry.

Tania had lost her mum to cancer just after she had turned fifteen. At the age of five she remembered her father beating up her mum one night. He had left her mother in a pool of blood and bolted away. He never came back. Up till this moment, Tania could not get her head around why daddy left.

Mum was a hardworking woman. She kept three jobs at a time to try to make ends meet. She had no education but she was determined that Tania would grow into a normal girl; she dreamt of Tania becoming a successful woman leading a happy life. But soon her life was cut short by the reality that she had brain cancer.

Tania soon became homeless and turned to the streets for survival. Men took advantage of her luck and forced her to do things for money. In drugs Tania found her only companion;

the only escape from the heartbreaks and pain that she had suffered.

On this night, as she spotted a childhood schoolmate laughing away with fellow students in the pub across the road, she remembered that she once had dreams. They were dreams of graduating from school and becoming a lawyer. She loved her mum so much. All she ever wanted to do was make mum proud. Back then she would dream with joy of how she was going to put a smile on her mother's face. Even when mum fought cancer and Tania was unable to continue with school, Tania tried her hands on other skills. From working at a bakery to hairdressing and auditioning for an acting role, she always got rejected. She was told that she just was not good enough. "Maybe this is why daddy left us", she would say to herself, "Maybe mum and I gave him nothing to be proud of". It seemed to her that for everything she tried to do, there were a thousand other people in the neighbourhood who could do it better.

"I probably was just aiming too high for myself", she thought. She was and would never be good enough to achieve such things. She remembered her ex-boyfriend used to say, "People like us were never meant to smell the roses". She had no reason to doubt him. This was life as Tania knew it.

The Mirror Principle

Tania was acting out a sad script; a script which all human beings are condemned to follow. What is this script? It is the things we learn from our days of childhood. Like in Tania's case, all human beings end up following a script. People tell you something about yourself long enough that you begin to believe it.

***

Life can be so mean when a child is surrounded by the wrong people. Tania represents millions of men and women who could have been successful but did not know any better. When people write you off long enough, you begin to believe that you are worth nothing. This is true; it is indeed a human thing. All humans are blessed with the gift of self-image. In the lives of many people, that gift has become a curse.

Our fulfilment is as high and as wide as our self-image. The mental perceptions we build for ourselves determine our goals and dreams; and in turn our fulfilment. Belief is everything but belief is mainly built in the subconscious mind. Hence we hardly have control over our fate if we have failed to control our beliefs.

So far we have talked about belief as though it was always within our control. The truth is it was never under our control in the first few years of our lives. For every one of us without exception, there was a time in our lives when we had little or no control over what we believed. We owe our beliefs, our self-esteem, and our views in life largely to the people whom we came in contact with during the most crucial period in a person's life: The formative years of Childhood; that golden age between the time of birth and the age of fifteen.

The Formative Years

What many parents fail to realise is that a child is a pure slate when he or she is born. Parents have given life to a brand new living creature with no previous history. If humans were books, a child would be an open book with plain pages. At birth, children have no opinions, no fears and no beliefs. A child is a clean slate upon which a new line is written for every passing moment of life. With every word they hear, every action they see, and every event they come in contact with, a new line is inscribed on their minds. As they grow older these lines turn to pages and from pages to books; volumes that are well compartmentalized in the libraries of their minds.

We know that as children grow older into adolescence and further into adulthood they gain more control over their beliefs and how they process information. However at these latter stages, their core beliefs are already formed from years of experience. Life constantly floods children with information. They very quickly turn from clean slates to vessels overflowing with information.

The crucial point to make here is that the years that tend to start forming our character are the years during which we have the least control over our lives. As a baby, a person cannot determine whom he or she meets, or the actions he or she sees, and consequently the beliefs he or she forms. Many psychologists agree that the formative years of an average child are between ages zero and fifteen. After these years some core beliefs are built which are nearly impossible to erase. Indeed more beliefs are built after the formative years but these latter perceptions always find their foundations on the core beliefs. It is a sobering thought to know that when a child starts getting control of his or her life, their core beliefs are already formed by then. Everything else aligns with the opinions garnered from the formative years.

A Mother's Words

Anyone who understands the value of life would likely appreciate the essence of parenthood; especially of motherhood. There are many professions in life. Of all the professions, the most daunting of them may well be parenthood.

To be clear, parenthood is not restricted to being the biological father or mother of a child. The true essence of parenthood includes any act that involves devoting resources to the development of a child. So whether you are a mother, father, aunt, uncle, foster parent, Godparent or teacher, you engage in some degree of parenting. Parenting is a profession. You are in the world's oldest profession; as long as you have children under your care.

Parenting is an art; a duty we owe to the children who are under our care. We should give credit to a man who builds a house and to the professionals whose efforts help to expand the frontiers of man's existence. Yet the highest honour should go to the men and women who devote some of their lives to form the character and shape the destinies of another human being.

Denzel Washington the famous actor is a testament to the influence of a mother. When at the age of fourteen Denzel lost contact with his father, he became a restless teenager. He was soon spending most of his time on the streets. It was a period of great struggle. Young Denzel was caught between leading a listless life on the streets without pressures, and finding the discipline to focus on his gifts. His mother was a constant source of motivation. She helped him to build character. She showed him love, direction, and possibilities. She worked hard at her local beauty parlour to support her children. She made sure that Denzel and his siblings attended school rather than resign to the world of hopelessness that engulfed many fatherless black children at the time.

She made him aware of his abilities and encouraged him to pursue his dreams. Today Denzel's dream of becoming a successful actor has been achieved. His mother was an unwavering pillar of support during the years he dithered on his life's journey. Looking back, Denzel said of his mother, "She never gave up on me. I messed up in school so much they were always sending me home but my mother always sent me right back". The success story of Denzel with the help of a determined mother becomes even more pronounced when we find out that the friends he once hung out with on the streets have all either been killed, or have served jail terms for various crimes.

Pablo Picasso once reminisced about the strength he drew from his mother. She impressed on young Pablo that he was cut out for greatness. Those words formed a pillar upon which he ascended to the hallowed ranks of artistic prominence. "My mother said to me, Son, if you become a soldier you will be a General; if you become a monk you will become the Pope. I became a painter and I wound up as Picasso". These were the reflections of Pablo Picasso. His mother's inspiring words sowed the seeds of self-belief for which Picasso would be greatly remembered.

Why Is Childhood So Vital?

Childhood is vital because it is the learning stage for all human beings. Learning continues all through life but it is the events of the formative years that form our character. Proper care at childhood is necessary for many reasons. Firstly there is physical and mental health. Secondly, each passing event, no matter how small, builds a layer of belief in the child's mind. Thirdly, a child does not have full control over his or her life. Until the age when society considers them as adults they pretty much bend to the dictates of the authorities in their lives.

A child lives at the mercy of his or her parents for most of the formative years. To the parent this becomes a great responsibility. As a parent, you are literally gifted with a book upon which to write a story. Whether that story turns out to be good or bad is very much up to you. Children's characters are a tribute to their parents; what they grow to become are the parent's true legacy. Many parents lament that they never had the chance to share their inner wealth with the world. Such parents forget that the blessing of birthing a child offers them the opportunity to leave their mark in life.

FACT

1. Studies have proven that the capacity for emotions like joy, fear, shyness, and happiness are already present at birth. However the way a child is nurtured shapes the way these emotions are developed.
2. Recent research proves that humans learn at the fastest pace during the first five years of their lives. A child's brain development is first formed during the first few years. Experiences that happen after the early years only build upon the foundations already laid.
3. Studies in the field of child psychology show that children who were nurtured with a high quality of care in their early years are several times less likely to exhibit anti-social behaviour. They are more likely to show higher levels of scholarly interest, language development, and cognitive development.

4. Medical examinations show that negative experiences at an early age have a lasting effect. Child abuse has been proven to inhibit brain development. Also, children exposed to violence are very likely to display violent and self-destructive behaviour later in life.

Children are like sponges. They soak up everything from their surroundings. The more soaked they become the less they are capable of taking in. It is important that the very first experiences they take in are encounters that positively affect them. Virtually all criminals have their distorted adult lives pointing back to negative childhood experiences. The environment that a child is brought up in is of crucial significance.

Affluence and nation of birth are factors that affect a child's outlook in life, but they are not as powerful as the signals received from the surrounding people and events. If dad and mum or those around the child have dominant thoughts of misfortune, the child would grow up with the belief that misfortune is normal and fortunate incidents are not meant for him or her. If a child is constantly exposed to negative events on social media the child will store these thoughts; in time the child forms a negative character.

The Mirror Principle

Again in human relations the transference of energy is always present. This is more so for a child. By virtue of infancy, a child possesses an insatiable capacity to receive. We all see the mannerisms that children pick up. They are quite funny to observe. What is even more amazing is the amount of energy they take in. Like a smoker who takes on the fragrance of a cigarette, so does a child take on the energy of his or her environment. As we now know, our subconscious learns things that we are not even aware of. The subconscious takes on emotions and beliefs from the things and events that the child is exposed to. This materializes into dominant thought, and soon the child's outlook to life is formed.

This phenomenon ties in with the results of research performed by sociologists on other animals. Now the eagle is one of the most versatile birds out there. Sociologists placed a newborn eagle among poultry to grow in the midst of chickens. For all its infancy the eagle behaved like a chicken. The eagle was unaware of its immense abilities. It knew no better. Its environment had conditioned it. Even when it sees another eagle in the sky, it may wish to be like the eagle but it chooses to live as a chicken. It has the character of a chicken, and that is its fate.

In today's world, it is impossible to perfectly guide a child so that the child is exposed to only positive energy. He or she will be exposed to both positive and negative forms of energy. How the child turns out will show the balance of experience. No parents could possibly protect a child from every kind of negativity, but it is the duty of the parent to create an environment where positive thoughts thrive. Again parents are only human and they would unintentionally teach the child the vices of selfishness, fear, and doubts but it is their duty to ensure that the balance of power favours positivity and healthy habits in the life of the child.

A child, like all other humans, lives according to The Mirror Principle. Nonetheless, until at a certain age, the child does not understand The Mirror Principle, and is unable to use it to his or her advantage. The parent on the other hand exerts some degree of influence over the child's life. Until the child becomes fully independent of the parents, the child continues to look up to the parent for guidance, comfort, and knowledge.

So will the child end up on the wrong side or right side of The Mirror Principle? Will the child find fulfilment, or meet with misery? The key to these outcomes is in the hands of none other than the parents. Let us quickly go through the three-fold duty of a parent to his or her child in relation to The Mirror Principle.

The Mirror Principle

"Your Perception of Your Potential is Your Reality"
The Mirror Principle

Help The Child to Nurture His Seed of Purpose

Every child is born with abilities. From an early age some abilities can be spotted. It is important for you as a parent to study your child and identify his or her strengths. Earlier in this book we stressed that one of the key ways of identifying your seed is recollecting the things you were interested in as a child. This is because childhood is a period of innocence. During childhood we express ourselves more freely and without prejudice. Oblivious to us but obvious to others, some things come easy for us. Where others struggle and retreat we perform with grace.

It is important to spot these abilities in a child and help them to protect it. Abilities are like fire. At infancy, they need to be fanned to flame. Soon enough they get so powerful that they become unstoppable. This is because the basic unit of ability is thought. Thoughts are only developed when they are encouraged and attended to. This is why abilities are symbolized as seeds. The easiest way to kill a plant is in its infancy; that tender state of fragility where the seed is at the mercy of everything around it; the phase of least resistance. Once a seed is developed, it begins to take root in the ground. Soon it shoots out as a firm plant; able to fend for itself and withstand its environment.

Any parent who does not believe that every child is born with a unique ability hampers the growth of that child. Growth is not only demonstrated in an increase in height or knowledge. True growth is also measured by how much positive knowledge and ability a child has gained. Even little things that appear insignificant but are good for the child should be encouraged. It is the little thoughts and acts of goodness that create a good character.

Some parents fall into the trap of imposing the abilities they want to see on a child. They ignore the abilities that the child seems to be better at. Establishing a successful life for a child does not mean imposing your wishes on the child; it means finding their passions and abilities and aiding the child to make the best of these gifts. Imagine what the world would have lost if the parents of Bill Gates had remained adamant and insisted that he should pursue a legal career. At that time, computers were of little economic value. The temptation must have been huge for them to write off the interest of their child in programming as a hopeless habit. They allowed him to develop his abilities and today he has pioneered the world into a computer age that has changed the face of human existence.

Sages Elixir

"Do not train a child to learn by force or harshness; but direct them to it by what amuses their minds, so that you may be better able to discover with accuracy the peculiar bent of the genius of each."

Plato

"The child must know that he is a miracle, that since the beginning of the world there hasn't been, and until the end of the world there will not be, another child like him."

Pablo Casals

Seeds come through in different forms. While some children's abilities are obvious, there are some who have the special gifts of imagination and passion. These are the dreamers. These children can see beyond the present circumstances. They see visions of themselves doing great things. These visions are not mere night dreams. A dream to such a child is the fulfilment of a dear cause. Such children display a unique passion for certain areas of human endeavour.

They have a passionate interest in something that drives them. It is that thing which makes their eyes to light up; the activity they seem forever drawn towards.

As a parent you should support a child's interests. Allow a child to dream. Do not mock a child's dreams. Indeed their dreams are often unrealistic and out of touch with adult wisdom, but we must never forget that many of the things we enjoy today were once mocked at; they were subjects of ridicule by parents and experts many years ago. Dreamers are often mocked, but you should be your child's number one fan. Help children to embellish their dreams; not to forget them.

A child's seed is a raw material. The parent is blessed with the vantage point of experience. The parent can use experience to develop this raw material and produce a valuable gem. From the wisdom that comes with age, a good parent knows how to apply just the right amount of pressure to a child's seed. With too much or too little pressure the seed could be destroyed; ability could be ruined and the world is robbed yet again.

It is true that for a child to be fully functional in life the child needs to be trained in some essential disciplines. The child needs to learn to communicate; the child needs to understand the merits of good social behaviour. The child needs outlets to burn his or her energies; children should not be denied the joys of the playground. The child needs to learn etiquette, history, language, and many more skills. All of these skills should only serve to support the one burning flame that lights up the child's life; the seed; the child's passions. This is his or her one true shot at finding fulfilment in life that the child should not be denied.

Sages Elixir

"Keep love in your heart. A life without it is like a sunless garden when the flowers are dead. The consciousness of loving and being loved brings a warmth and a richness to life that nothing else can bring."

Oscar Wilde

Mould The Child's Beliefs

A parent does not have much control over what kind of seed of purpose a child possesses. However there is one thing the parent is largely responsible for: The child's beliefs. Humans are products of belief. What a person believes the person ultimately becomes. A person who inherits great riches but believes he or she is poor soon becomes poor. Likewise a person oblivious of her or her disadvantages, and driven by thoughts of success would usually succeed. A child's mind starts off as a clean slate. Every moment that passes by, the child learns of things to fear, things to cherish, things to respect, and things to hate. Through the daily reception of knowledge, beliefs are built in a child.

The crucial aspect of belief is that a person's character is wholly established on their beliefs or their outlook in life. The nobility of a person's mind finds its substance in what they have been taught since birth. Beliefs determine character. Character manifests itself in actions. Our actions determine our fate. In essence, a person's belief is his or her fate. There is no gainsaying that a child's values will be tested at every point in life. The choices the child makes are a clear reflection of the child's values. Parents are largely responsible for these values. If a child is raised to treat certain groups of people with disdain, the child knows no better and would act accordingly. When a teenager grabs a knife and takes the life of another human being, it is evidence of the little value the teenager places on human life.

Let us remind ourselves of the definition of a parent in the context of this book. A parent is not only the biological father or mother of a child. A parent is anybody whose immediate duty it is to look after the affairs of a child. A parent is more than a person; it is an office. Parenthood is not a specific task for specific persons; it is a shared responsibility. Therefore a schoolteacher assumes the role of a parent once that child enters into the four walls of the school. A nanny, godparent, grandparents or foster parents all take the role of parent at one point or another in a child's life. In a sense all adults tend to assume this role from time to time.

In building a child's beliefs, it is the parent's duty to ensure that a child forms the right beliefs, and hence the right values. So how does a child establish beliefs? The simple answer is through contact. Children create beliefs through the people and events they come in contact with. Let us take an example. Jimmy is three years old. The only way he knows to stop doing anything is by being smacked and yelled at. To get him or his siblings to stop playing after bedtime, or stand still at the pedestrian traffic lights, he would normally take a beating from his uncle, aunt, dad, or mum. As he grows older he observes at home that a punch or two can quickly settle every conflict or argument. He learns that the one who hits another seems to have his way. Now Jimmy is in his late forties. He has been arrested yet again on charges of physical assault. The man knows no better. As a child he learnt that hitting others helps you to win a cause. His belief was wrong and self-destructive; they controlled his actions.

There are thousands of other people who grew up in the same environment as Jimmy but have not behaved in a similar fashion. Why is this? Again the answer to this is not farfetched. In the case of these people, they have come in contact with conflicting information. This information educated them on the values of respect for others; it taught them the consequences of assault. Their beliefs therefore tilted to the side of restraint over aggression; courtesy over disrespect. This positive information could have come from any of many sources. It could have come from school, church, a positive television program, a good book, siblings and much more. The world is filled with many things that could positively or negatively influence a child. The balance of power lies in the hands of the parent.

The parent should ensure that the exposures that influence the child the most are both positive and civil. Soon a child learns that almost every situation in life presents themselves with two distinct options: an unethical shortcut, or the moral high ground. The child should truly believe that the key to fulfilment often takes us through the road less travelled. It is at this height of learning that a child's character is polished into a fine, unbreakable gem.

Now how does this all relate to The Mirror Principle? Remember that The Mirror Principle acts based on dominant thought. If the dominant thought is failure, no matter how strong the potential is, the child is headed for failure. All humans gravitate towards their most dominant thought. Dominant thought often finds its roots in the beliefs established at childhood.

As an influential figure on a child's belief patterns, you should make children know that success is their right and not the reserve of a chosen few. You should make them see the glass as half full and not half empty. Instil in them the spirit of abundance rather than the scarcity mentality. Indeed they should understand that defeat must come sometimes, and that prudence is needed for progress to happen. Nonetheless success should be their final destination; an honest fulfilment of their ultimate goal. One of the key beliefs I gained in childhood and for which I am eternally grateful is how to treat the desire to win. My motto was "Truly always aim to win and if you lose, try to enjoy the humour in losing". It is good to win but losing can be turned from a tragedy to a comedy. There are lessons to be learnt from a defeat but loads of humour too. The reason losing was an experience I could laugh over was because I knew that for everything in life, there are a thousand more opportunities. Anytime I was going for an interview or taking a test I would repeat that motto to myself. I believed it; and because it is the truth I have never been worse off for believing it. Such beliefs make life fun even while you wait. Protect your child from the virus of scarcity mentality.

Sages Elixir

"Genius is no more than childhood recaptured at will, childhood equipped now with man's physical means to express itself, and with the analytical mind that enables it to bring order into the sum of experience, involuntarily amassed."

Charles Baudelaire

The sage Abraham Lincoln wrote and delivered a legendary note to the teacher of his son. As you read these lines you come in contact with a man's love for his young son. Also he provides simple but powerful tenets which if applied in the upbringing of any child, could do the child a lot of good. Here is an abridged version of the note that is now commonly referred to as the Letter of Abraham Lincoln To His Son's Teacher.

"He will have to learn, I know, that all men are not just, all men are not true. But teach him also that for every scoundrel there is a hero; that for every selfish politician, there is a dedicated leader. Teach him for every enemy there is a friend. Teach him that a dollar earned is far more valuable than five found. Teach him to learn to lose and also to enjoy winning.

The Mirror Principle

Teach him, if you can the wonder of books. But also give him quiet time to ponder the eternal mystery of birds in the sky, bees in the sun, and the flowers on a green hillside. In the school teach him, it is far more honourable to fail than to cheat. Teach him to have faith in his own ideas even if everyone tells him they are wrong...

Teach him to be gentle with gentle people, and tough with the tough. Try to give my son the strength not to follow the crowd when everyone is getting on the bandwagon...Teach him to listen to all men but teach him also to filter all he hears on a screen of truth and take only the good that comes through.

Teach him if you can, how to laugh when he is sad...Teach him there is no shame in tears, Teach him to scoff at cynics and to beware of too much sweetness...Teach him to sell his brawn and brain to the highest bidders but never to put a price-tag on his heart and soul.

Teach him to close his ears to a howling mob; and to stand and fight if he thinks he's right. Treat him gently, but do not cuddle him, because only the test of fire makes fine steel. Let him have the courage to be impatient...let him have the patience to be brave. Teach him always to

have sublime faith in himself, because then he will have sublime faith in mankind.
This is a big order but see what you can do…He is such a fine little fellow, my son!"

You Are The Child's Mirror

The Mirror Principle in our lives often starts with our childhood beliefs. The Mirror Principle in a child's life starts with the parent. You are the child's mirror; the child's hope for a better future; the child's trusted star; the child's guiding light. It is true that when the independence of adulthood sets in we are able to use our mirror to make judgements by ourselves. Yet when we rewind several years back to those formative years, we realize that the only mirrors we ever knew as children were our parents. We saw ourselves through their eyes; we hung on to every word that fell from their lips.

A parent's influence is far reaching. It is amazing how much children pick up from their parents. They see in their parents an example of how life should be lived. Until they start getting exposure to other forms of media, or become fully independent they look to their parents as the model of how to

The Mirror Principle

respond to life's challenges. Whether that example is good or bad is totally determined by the parents.

Some noteworthy researchers have proven that a child is likely to be shaped more by peers than by parents. While this is true, it is important to remember that the peers the child gets exposed to are determinable by the parents. The school the child attends, the neighbourhood the child grows up in, and the friends the child gets introduced to could be highly influenced by the parent. In essence a parent controls the available examples that a child can emulate.

The mirror is the child's self-image; their mental perception of who they are. The approval or disapproval of the parent has a lasting effect on a child's perception of self. A parent's words of commendation or rebuke are mirrored on the child's self-image. A child puts so much trust in the parent that even when they have an amazing skill or interest, they have no mental image of the great persons they could become. For this reason, a parent should consciously work towards encouraging the child and showing that child their true greatness.

When the mirror of greatness is upheld long enough for the child to see, the magic of the mirror will begin to materialize. Soon the child transforms from an insecure infant to a confident youth; a clueless child to a focused adult. In a sense the parent sets the bar for what the child can achieve. Children rarely go over that bar; they hardly progress beyond the mirror image they see in their parent's eyes and hear from their parent's words. To a large extent, the parent draws the pictures; the child merely colours it.

It is true that the ones who hurt us the most are those who are closest to us. The bond of relationship breeds trust; and trust makes us lose grounds. To the ones we trust, we yield to their perceptions; we reveal parts of our nakedness to them. This is the reason why it hurts when those closest to us attack our dreams. We think they know; we feel that to an extent what they say may be true. This hurt is never more pronounced than when a parent attacks a child's purpose.

Parents should not shy away from using reinforcers to help the child remain focused. A lot of things fight for the child's attention so it is vital to surround him or her with as many reinforcers as one can find. Like compassion, reinforcers can never be too many. Parents could replicate the image in the mirror through the use of inspirational books, past achievements, meaningful movies, inscriptions, and many more.

Speaking of past achievements, there is a wealth of good in displaying trophies, certificates, or medals won by a child in obvious areas around the home. Anytime children see these testaments of success they are subtly reminded of who they are, and what they could achieve. These reinforcers are small but mighty signals that shape the course of a child's life.

The Mirror Principle in a child's life is simply captured thus:

> *"The child's Belief in his or her Potential shall become the child's Reality"*
>
> *The Mirror Principle*

If the child's potentials are developed but beliefs are weak, the child's reality is one of disappointment. If the child's beliefs are strong but potentials are undeveloped at childhood, then the child's reality is one of frustration. Ideally if the child's beliefs are strong and potentials are developed, the child's reality is filled with fulfilment in its truest form.

Nutshell

Have you ever tried to pull on an elastic band? No matter how much you pull on it, the band returns back to its original shape. Such is the mind of many adults. Psychologists have come to some level of conclusion that the mental development of any person meets with greater resistance and scrutiny after the formative years from birth to teenage years.

Learning never stops; adult lives can still be transformed; yet the perceptions built in the formative years are hard to overturn. It takes years to overcome the blocks of knowledge that we pick up during those formative years. For this reason childhood is vital to everyone's success.

Indeed we have seen men and women with distorted childhoods who use The Mirror Principle to rebuild their lives and achieve fulfilment. However, these persons will testify of the years wasted in unlearning the wrong things they picked up during those detrimental childhood years.

A child is a clean slate at birth. Every passing moment, the child takes a new thought onboard. These incoming thoughts tilt the balance for or against the child's purpose. There are no such things as ineffectual thoughts. All thoughts carry power. A single thought may not do much on its own but when thoughts come together they could form a dominant force. Thoughts create beliefs and beliefs are very hard to change.

A parent is not a person; it is a role. A parent is anyone saddled with the responsibility of looking after a child at any given point in time. Parenting is an art; perhaps the most crucial profession in our lives. Through parenting we give life to a purpose and we partly determine the outcome of another person's existence. All human beings have a mirror in their minds, and children are not exempt. Unlike adults, their mirrors hold the image they see in the mirror held up by their parents. Every child seeks direction from parents. Every child, no matter how gifted, needs the confidence that comes from a parent's acknowledgement of the child's gifts. Children are often dreamers and they need the help of their parents to keep these dreams alive. Every child has a right to a happy life, and they need their parents to create that environment.

10 The Conclusion Of The Matter

In 1954 an article was published in the Readers Digest magazine. It was based on a true story. It is one of those real-life events we often explain away as a coincidence. Then again, when we pause to ponder over real events like this one, the true essence of our existence comes alive to us. Let us forget about the computers, the gadgets and the cosmetics for a moment. Let us forget about the bills, the need to look beautiful, and the hustle to survive. Let us remind ourselves of who we truly are, and why we are here. It is only in doing so that our lives find its fulfilment. Only in the hallowed chambers of these noble thoughts do we realise how connected we are; one to another.

It was four days to Christmas. A young church pastor in Brooklyn, New York was left to sort out the ruins of his church after a devastating storm. The pastor and his wife had toiled for months to get the church ready and in time for the yuletide. They had hoped they could hold an inaugural service on

Christmas Eve. However the weather had other plans. The storm had left a large hole in the wall behind the pulpit. It so happened that a beautiful handmade tablecloth was being sold at a nearby charity event. The pastor bought the tablecloth and improvised a cover for the wall.

As the pastor hung the tablecloth over the wall he noticed an older woman had just missed her bus. He knew it would take another forty-five minutes before the next bus showed up. It had also begun to snow. He invited the woman into the church to get warm. At first she paid no attention but when she took a look at the tablecloth that the pastor had just finished hanging, the sight of it made her shudder. The tablecloth was the same one she had made thirty-five years ago back home in Austria.

She explained to the pastor how she and her husband had led a wealthy life in Austria before the Nazis arrived. Her husband did not support the Nazis so they were forced to flee. She fled first with her husband to follow the week after. It did not go to plan. She got captured and sent to prison. She heard that her husband was also captured, and had died in a concentration camp. The woman made the pastor keep the tablecloth, and he insisted on giving her a lift home. It turned out she lived on Staten Island and was only in Brooklyn on the day for a housecleaning job.

On Xmas eve, the service went ahead successfully. An older man approached the pastor at the end of the service. The man looked stunned as he asked about the origin of the tablecloth. He explained that the tablecloth was identical to the one his wife had made many years ago. They had both lived in Austria. He was captured before he could make his way to her during the war. He had not seen her for thirty-five years. The astounded pastor insisted on taking the man for a ride into town. He drove to Staten Island, and they headed straight for the same house he had been the day before to drop off the older lady. Right there he witnessed the happiest Christmas reunion he could ever imagine.

Real stories like this wake us up to the fact that there are many little things that connect us together. As a race we have made giant strides in understanding our environment but there is a lot more to discover. There are events not immediately visible to us that affect us greatly. Like the couple in the tablecloth story, we do not know how important the little things we do today could become in the future. Every day we should wake up with a positive and inquisitive mind. This goes beyond a curiosity for how the stock markets will fare, what the weather holds, or the latest social gossip. We should remind ourselves of the value of all things; even the little things like a handmade tablecloth. We should remind ourselves of those who love us and those we love. We should remind ourselves of what we live for, and why we cherish the things we hold dear. Every day we should add to what we know about our environment, our history, and ourselves. Thus at the end of life's sojourn we could look back with a feeling of ultimate fulfilment.

As you add to your knowledge, you do yourself a world of good to remember these three things and their place in your life: The Seed, The Mirror, and The Mind. They are the pillars of your life. Your life runs on one powerful principle: The Mirror Principle. The Seed, the Mirror, and the Mind are the three pillars on which The Mirror Principle operates. Whether you are aware of it or not, like all natural laws, The Mirror Principle will bring results into your life. The kind of results you get is determined by how you use these three pillars.

"Your Perception of Your Potential is Your Reality"
The Mirror Principle

The seed is your purpose. It is your dream; your passion or the ability that makes you stand out. For a few persons their seed is obvious for all to see. Yet to many of us we have to dig deep to unearth our seed. Nonetheless there is a seed of purpose lying inside every one of us. No one can take that seed away from us. The seed is connected to our minds. Negative people could place fetters on our physical bodies, but they cannot place fetters on our minds except for when we allow them. Even when we have been naive and have allowed negative people to place barriers in our minds, we always have the immediate power to get back on track. Your seed has its place in the world. No matter who is out there or what others think. Your seed is your gift to the world. It carries a stamp of your uniqueness, which makes it forever original. It was there in your childhood, and even when you fail to recognize it, your seed is loyal till the end. You could be living in the last few years of your life, but it is never too late to unleash your seed on the world.

The Mirror is not just another man-made invention. Before the ancient Egyptians made mirrors from polished copper, man has always been blessed with the gift of the mirror. Right from the days when men and women would stand before a pool of water to observe their own reflections the mirror has existed. The mirror tells you who you are. It controls how you see yourself. It is the creator of your self-image. The mirror that affects your life the most is not the looking glass on your bedroom wall. It is the mental mirror; the mirror which resides in the minds of all human beings. The mirror's strongest attribute is its transformative power. Mirrors possess the ability

The Mirror Principle

to transform which supersedes their ability to reflect. Our mental mirror image dictates what we do, how we act, and where we go. In essence it transforms us to become what we see of ourselves. Like the seed the mirror is connected to the mind; it is totally under your control.

The Mind is a powerhouse. It is what we are. Indeed the seed and the mirror are part of the mind. In the context of The Mirror Principle, the mind represents our beliefs. We have seen that the basic units of the mind are thoughts. These thoughts are arranged in a highly sophisticated manner. Emotions, beliefs and memories are different forms of thought all linked together in our minds by the events that we go through. The thoughts we dwell on with our deepest emotions or with the most frequency soon become our dominant thoughts; thoughts which remain active even while we are asleep. Thoughts are a form of energy. They interact with everything else in the universe. Through our thoughts we interact with the universal process of transference of energy. We obey the laws of attraction through our thoughts. It is true that we cannot attract things simply by wishing for them, but we surely attract things into our lives when we allow the thoughts of them to dominate our minds. These dominant thoughts drive our actions and hence our results. Our mind is a potent force.

The Mirror Principle is a natural law. It is as old as mankind. There are thousands of decisions that we make on a daily basis. Sometimes we are only aware of a few hundred of these decisions. Most of the decisions we take are done involuntarily. We may not know when we make these decisions or act accordingly but they affect our direction in life. They are based on our belief systems. They are built from a heap of thoughts we have entertained in the past; thoughts which turn around to make or break us.

The Mirror Principle is as simple as it is powerful. It says your reality is a product of your perception and your seed. In simple terms, it says your situation is dictated by your actions and decisions, which are based on your beliefs and self-image. It all starts with the mirror. The perception you have of yourself impacts how you see everything. You then form your perception on everything, and inevitably create your reality. Your perception of your goals determines whether you would achieve them or not. If this perception is focused on the gifts you have within you, achievement is not far away. The greatness of your achievement is determined by how positive your mirror is.

The Mirror Principle can be used to attain fulfilment in life. The first thing it requires is the right mirror image of who you want to become. Next it requires you to discover what you were born to do. Thirdly and lastly, it requires you to focus your mental energy on the image within the mirror. The Mirror Principle takes care of the rest. The Mirror Principle creates your reality based on the image you see.

One of the most profound discoveries in life is perhaps one of the simplest facts of life: You determine your ultimate fate simply by the perception you create of yourself and of everything else. Create your mirror, and it will turn around to create you. Find and harness your seed of purpose, and it will yield you a beautiful garden. It will take you beyond the realm of accomplishment, and into the realm of fulfilment.

The life of every individual, nation, organization, or child, is lived based on The Mirror Principle. We do ourselves a tremendous favour when we become conscious of this principle. By knowing how The Mirror Principle operates in our lives we could use it to our advantage. To master The Mirror Principle is to find a pathway to accomplishment. To employ the principle around your seed of purpose is to know fulfilment.

It is easy to fall to the pressures of daily living in today's world. It is even easier to succumb to the short-lived pleasures of aimless indulgence. Yet paying attention to your seed, your mirror, and your mind, yields benefits that are beyond description. The feeling of fulfilment beats any other pleasure or sense of happiness that there is. As you decide to take the road to fulfilment, you shall surely encounter challenges; hurdles that all things in motion have to overcome. It may require discipline but it is surely worth its rewards.

Life is a book. Let us not leave the ink of the chapters of our history in unused pens. The world has been robbed enough. Beyond our present circumstances there is a story in each and every one of us waiting to be told; masterpieces that we may not acknowledge, but they reside within us. We are all born with a seed of greatness. It is not about fame, gold medals, or platinum rings; it is about meeting the needs in other people's lives; that ultimate feeling of fulfilment. Your seed may meet the needs of thousands, or just a single person. Yet as long as you find that seed and apply yourself to it, yours shall be a life that knows fulfilment.

At the end of the day, after all is said and done, let us ensure that there is more done than said. You could refuse to be a common man or woman. It is your right to be uncommon if you can. It is your choice to prefer the changes of life to the safety of guaranteed existence; the thrill of fulfilment to the still and calm of Ethiopia. The mountains before you may be tough; they cannot get any tougher but you can. We have been blessed with the most audacious gift of all: The gift of imagination. With it we create our self-image, and then create

The Mirror Principle

a new life. The day imagination ceases is the same day that we all truly die. Indeed all things are possible to those that believe.

"Your Perception of Your Potential is Your Reality"
The Mirror Principle

Every now and then, a book is released that reminds us of what truly makes us great. The Mirror Principle rekindles the human torch; lest we forget, in the midst of everything, that we were born great, and have a beautiful inheritance.

Tempted to say this book is a culmination of years of experience or great expertise. Alas, it is not. The Mirror Principle is frankly not new; its message has been delivered from generation to generation. This book only serves to make it reverberate. Its power is yours to own and enjoy.

Your mission is to use The Mirror Principle to write your own story in the sands of time. Your life is a book waiting to be read. Let us not leave the ink of the chapters of our history in unused pens. The world has been robbed enough.

Discover more content from The Mirror Principle and engage with other readers of the book on www.themirrorprinciple.org

Discover more stories..

Join us at www.publishwiz.com or follow us on Twitter @publishwiz to be part of a community of people with a passion for stories, good books and reading.

Books are one of the greatest gifts of our time; books inspire, teach and open our imagination to wondrous possibilities.

We hope our books will do just that for you.

www.publishwiz.com

@publishwiz

publishwiz

Printed in Great Britain
by Amazon